GREAT BOOKS
for High School Kids

GREAT BOOKS
for High School Kids

*A Teachers' Guide to Books
That Can Change Teens' Lives*

*Edited by
Rick Ayers and Amy Crawford*

BEACON
150

BEACON PRESS
BOSTON

BEACON PRESS
25 Beacon Street
Boston, Massachusetts 02108-2892
www.beacon.org

Beacon Press books are published under the auspices of
the Unitarian Universalist Association of Congregations.

07   8 7 6 5

This book is printed on acid-free paper that meets the uncoated paper
ANSI/NISO specifications for permanence as revised in 1992.

Text design by Joyce C. Weston
Composition by Wilsted & Taylor Publishing Services

Library of Congress Cataloging-in-Publication Data

Great books for high school kids : a teachers' guide to books that
can change teens' lives / edited by Rick Ayers, Amy Crawford. — 1st
pbk. ed.
    p. cm.
   Includes indexes.
   ISBN 0-8070-3255-7 (pbk. : alk. paper)
   1. High school students—Books and reading—United States.
2. Teenagers—Books and reading—United States. 3. American
literature—Study and teaching (Secondary)—United States.
4. Best books—United States.   I. Ayers, Rick. II. Crawford, Amy.
Z1039.H54G74   2004
028.5 '35—dc22   2003026369

We dedicate this book to our students—
past, present, and future—who change the way we
read great books.

CONTENTS

INTRODUCTION

Literature is no one's private ground. Literature is common ground; let us trespass freely and fearlessly and find our own way for ourselves.

—Virginia Woolf

As TEACHERS WHO LOVE to read and discuss great books with teenagers, we have long dreamed of a book that could serve as a map to the vast literary territory that we know teens can—but rarely do—explore. In the privacy of our classrooms, we love to watch our students falling under the spell of wonderful books. Some days a book hits right on the mark for an entire class, and the conversations get so exciting that we burst down our colleagues' doors, rave to our families, write in our journals, and eagerly anticipate returning to class the following day. Other days we feel lucky to direct the right student to the right book, and a month or a week or a day later we sit down together at lunch or after school and hash it out. These experiences make us feel privileged to do the work that we do. (After all, in what other profession do you get paid to read great books with interesting young people?) They also make us feel like spreading the word on what kids can make of books.

We know teenagers love reading great books—we've seen them do it. And this book is packed with stories about the thrill of reading and lists of books high school kids have responded to with delight, fascination, awe, affection, and fierce enthusiasm. Our recommendations are meant to be exploratory and to invite suggestions, not to set forth academic requirements, and certainly not the definitive list that will get kids into Yale. They are about reading for the joy of it, not reading for credentials. We also tell stories—classroom and personal and idiosyncratic stories. By telling the journey of our classrooms, we hope to evoke the power of these books so that teenagers can embark on their own adventures with books, with classmates, friends, parents, and teachers.

• WHAT WE BELIEVE ABOUT THE POWER OF BOOKS •

We come to this project as unabashed partisans. We believe in the power of books. We believe literature holds words that enrich—and even save—our lives. We believe writers write not to create difficult assignments for English class but often, at least, to convey something they figured out during a life of sacrifice, error, love, delight, boredom, frustration, and horror. The Greeks fought the Trojan War and then endured the bloody Peloponnesian War. They knew something of human folly and arrogance. They wrote stories down to figure things out for themselves; some of them also wrote them down for us, hoping we would lead better lives, make better choices.

Then again, we believe literature is there not only to give kids "the answer," and certainly not to deliver a message. Great books trigger questions—lots of questions, important questions. A book might stand witness to the fact that the lessons in life are not so easy or that people and nature are delightfully, maddeningly flawed.

We believe that literature is meant, as John Berger wrote, to "make the familiar strange." Great writing allows readers to look at their world in a new, wondrous, and engaged way. Literature gives them a new eye, a new innocence.

We believe that literature and life are connected. A book might introduce you to a character so similar to someone you've known that you unconsciously confuse the actions of the fictional character with those of a beloved friend. Another book might bring to life a character so compelling, so different from anyone you've known, and yet so real, that he joins the ranks of people you know and care about. Literature allows us to try on possible selves.

We believe that what you find in literature is often sheer beauty— the stunning mix of words and images, the resonant phrase—the same transcendent experience, the same elevation of feeling, that you might find in a favorite piece of music, a magnificent film, or a compelling painting.

We teachers sometimes make the mistake of assuming teenagers want to read about themselves in every book they open—that there is a narcissism in teen culture that we must pander to. In fact, most teens favor books that offer experiences far from their own—books that have them roaring across the frozen plains of Russia, dreaming of warm tea in front of the samovar, or discovering magical powers in Virginia. What we delight in—kids and adults alike—are books that expand our sensibilities and deepen our encounter with the world.

Literature is all around us. Book sales are higher than ever before. The walls of many homes are lined with books. But many folks learn, often in school, to be intimidated by literature; they fear "great literature" is encrypted in a secret code they never got access to. We hope this volume dispels the false notion that there is a society of in-the-know literary types who have a hold on the "right" way to read a book. By reading great books, everyone can enjoy fantastic new horizons on their own terms, in their own way. The more we read the more we realize that there is an almost infinite amount of information in the world, and we are always going to face the challenge, which books can uniquely help us with, of stitching together meaning, satisfaction, and fulfillment in our lives.

• WHAT'S A GREAT BOOK? •

We titled this book *Great Books for High School Kids* because we mean it. All the books we talk about here deserve the label "great." All of them have something that made them extraordinary to readers who love books: some are funny, others intense, and still others profound. What they have in common is that they all generated extraordinary reactions in readers we trust.

By "great books" we don't mean what some traditional cultural critics mean by that term. This is not a "what you need to know" book. We don't subscribe to the scolding approach of William Bennett or E. D. Hirsch. Great books are not the same as the "Great Books" demanded by the canon warriors, and we certainly don't see them as teaching neatly packaged moral lessons. We deliberately abstain from joining in the harsh debates between those who uphold the Western classics and those who denounce the "dead white men" in favor of texts by writers who are too often marginalized—authors from the Third World, women, and people of color. This is a war not worth waging, since we would all be diminished if either side won a decisive victory.

Wonderful writing exists on both sides of the trenches. And within our classrooms, students of all colors and representing all parts of the world make sense of great books by using the lenses created by the lives they lead, and they are broadened by the lenses of their peers and teachers. In a sense we are trying to reclaim "greatness" from the narrow attempts to define and confine it. We therefore include a number of books that are widely accepted as classics not only because many are truly wonderful books but also because many are so emphatically within the reach of high school kids. By "classics" we don't mean just the classics that—for particular reasons of history and thematic content—happen to get assigned in most high schools. Too often adults and institutions underestimate high school readers. We've seen unexpectedly challenging texts sweep kids up.

Even though the majority of the books are fiction—primarily novels and a few plays—in the middle of the process we decided that it just didn't make sense to ban other types of books. We have included a more limited selection of poetry and nonfiction that we highly recommend. We wouldn't sleep well at night knowing we had not extolled the wondrous magic of Neruda's poetry or McPhee's nature writing.

We claim no final authority for these lists. We extend our recommendations knowing full well that other authors and readers could come up with a different, interesting, and engaging list. We simply offer our enthusiasm and good cheer for the project.

• THE TEACHERS' ESSAYS •

To give kids a taste of what a great work can mean in an exciting classroom, this book is organized *first* around stories told by some very good teachers. It is teachers who often experience the excitement of connecting teenagers to great books. Many adults have dreary and dreaded memories of English class. Too often, we, high school English teachers, find ourselves slipping into the comfortable language of our specialization, recalling the excitement of our college "lit crit" classes but not working to connect the amazing books we are reading to the lives and minds of the kids we teach. We sought out stories of classrooms that look very different from the stereotypical image of a teacher "decoding" an abstruse text to a roomful of dutiful (or bored) students. Amazing things happen every day in classrooms where students are engaged in reading great books, and we believe that these stories offer individual readers who are independently exploring the world of books valuable and exciting ideas about how books can be read.

You will see some great teaching and learning going on here. This book is not, perhaps, what the Education Trust would like kids to study. It is not the scripted curriculum and test prep that are increasingly becoming the official way of schooling. The teachers whose stories follow practice what Neil Postman called "teaching as a subversive activity." Books, after all, can be dangerous. To get to the good stuff, to teach really well, teachers have to go off the official script, invent a curriculum, and embrace opportunities for a transformative education. These are the kinds of teachers who wrote the essays in this book.

Each essay is a particular story, one that happened at one time and in one place. Each story is indicative of a type of book that has been eye opening for many teens. We have stitched these stories together from our memories of the discussions, our journals, student writing, and student input. We have changed students' names, and sometimes, for the sake of clarity and privacy, we have conflated characters or simplified situations. But the fundamental journey, the experience among the students and the adult and the book, is rendered in its essence. And, because we live in the United States in the early-twenty-first century, issues of race, gender, power, and social ethics are contested territory arising in each situation.

We decided early on that we were not going to try to be representative, balanced, or consistent in our selection. Instead we wanted to create a quirky series of stories about a quirky set of books—some old, some new, some easily accessible, and others requiring a stretch. In the end, we narrowed the series down to these few pieces, essays that can stand as model journeys taken with wonderful books. These journeys are not definitive; they do not "explain" the book in some final way. In a different year, the authors of these essays would have told different stories. These are simply true stories about groups of students and teachers encountering great literature together. Ultimately, these stories show young people negotiating all the challenges that we face in our world.

• THE LISTS AND INDEXES •

While working on this project, we found out that people love lists. Perhaps there is something inherently fun about creating, sharing, and checking off lists. Nick Hornby played on our fascination for lists in his novel *High Fidelity*, which he began with a list of his five worst breakups and then filled with lists of perfect songs for particular situations. We have found lists to be a big hit among our students, too. They love writing that involves justifying selections on a "top 10 list," and they eagerly add to lists of recommended books we circulate.

Everyone loves remembering books that changed their lives. When we tell people about our project, they start reminiscing about books that blew them away as kids, and the next thing you know you can't get them to stop talking. When we ask our students to make a list of books that have changed their lives, works that have made them who they are today, each kid creates a unique list that is sacred and resonant with meaning. They argue about each other's inclusions and add to their own upon hearing a forgotten title. Think of the lists as an extended, animated conversation.

We have tried to organize the lists in a way that is conducive to getting this conversation going. Following each essay you will find two book lists that connect with the work discussed in the essay in different ways. The idea is for each work to suggest myriad others along various paths. So if the essay on *Bless Me, Ultima* (see chapter 5) turns you on to spiritual journeys, then you can try out *The Bone People*, a spiritual journey set in New Zealand, and *Siddhartha*, another set in India. But if it was the father-son relationship that made *Bless Me, Ultima* memorable for you, you might rather check out *A River Runs through It* or *This Boy's Life*, which you'll find under "Parents, Imperfect."

Although we concede that great writing defies categorization, we want to give young readers who may be unfamiliar with many of our choices the chance to browse confidently in a variety of directions. To help them with this process, we have compiled indexes at the back of the book in which each book is cross-referenced by genre, the author's background, and subgenre. For instance, James Baldwin's *Giovanni's Room* is listed in the chapter on *Huckleberry Finn* as an example of "talking back" or questioning authority, but it is also a classic book of gay fiction as well as a leading example of African American literature. Our subindexes, intended to be both playful and practical, include books that came to us primarily recommended by teens, big fat books to take on a road trip, and books that have laughter in the title. We don't claim to be exhaustive in our categorization, but we have tried to open rather than close doors.

Creating these lists was an adventure. We spent the last year collecting stories about favorite books from students and their parents, colleagues, friends, librarians, and strangers. And they are still, of course, supremely incomplete. We are confident that the titles listed here represent great books, but the universe of great books is large. We don't claim to be definitive because we don't believe any list can be. We do, however, claim to be interesting.

We invite teens to add other suggestions to the list. We will maintain a Web page, found at www.beacon.org, which will include other essays, comments on the books mentioned here, and suggestions for new ones. Join the conversation!

• HOW TO USE THIS BOOK •

We want to be clear: this book is not just for teachers. We put this volume together to help teenagers discover books that they might love, as well as to invite adults to dig in to the same process—for themselves and for the young adults in their lives. This book is the beginning of a conversation, one of equals at different stages in the journey; it is a jumping-off point to a delightful discussion about, and relationship with, literature.

There is no one "right" way to read this book—no matter how old you are. We imagine some will find it fun to curl up with, and others will primarily browse, dipping in and referring back to it later. To invite you to use it in multiple ways, we've tried to provide many avenues into the book.

For example, you can start with the essays. Read the experiences of kids talking about and living with these books, and see what strikes you. Read the book they read. How does your experience compare and contrast with theirs? Does their journey suggest ways of reading other books, questions you might want to ask of other books, things you might want to find out?

Or you can examine the main list and find what interests you. Find a book that you have loved in the title index provided at the back of this volume, and see where it appears in the main body of the list. What other books surround it? Where does your eye land? Where does that book lead you?

Sometimes the grouping of books may lead you to make unexpected connections. You might be looking at books about young people struggling to make something of themselves and discover *Hoop Dreams*—then you might check out other African American books and discover the mystery writer Chester Himes. You might start at Kenzaburo Oe's horrific and redeeming Japanese novel of abandoned youth in *Nip the Buds, Shoot the Kids* and, via the list of alienation and outsiders, end up at Gogol's classic *Dead Souls*.

We know that many teachers will find inspiration from classroom tales of colleagues as well as from the lists. The book may help to shake up reading lists around the country—since teachers, in choosing books to teach, often have much more latitude than they are aware of. We also hope parents will find books to recommend to their kids or to read along with them. And finally, of course, we hope teens will explore the lists and the worlds they represent on their own, beginning a practice that can be one of the most rewarding in life—the practice of independent reading.

We take seriously the Virginia Woolf quotation at the beginning of this introduction. Literature is no one's private territory. Pick up a book. Give it a chance. When possible, write in the book. Underline. Put exclamation points, question marks, and comments in the margins. (Use a pencil if this makes you uncomfortable.) When you find yourself at a standstill, feel free to put the book down and try another. Part of the spirit of this book is that many choices await you. If one book isn't working for you, chances are there's another one out there that will. When you discover a writer you love, read everything she wrote. (This works especially well with poetry! You'll find you "get" it on a whole new level.) Then find out what she likes to read and what she grew up reading, and give that a try.

Finally, we hope this book inspires people to read together—not only teachers with students, but groups of kids and families as well. Create reading communities by starting a book group, passing around a journal, or simply making time for book talk with friends or over dinner. If you are a parent, buy two copies of a book and arrange to read books together with your son or daughter. If you are a teen, you can find a reading community in your classmates, your teacher, your family, your friends, and even someone you encounter on the Internet or in the book review section.

One of the paradoxes of great literature is that it is supremely individual and yet collective. Literature is not a solitary journey. We are always accompanied by thousands of authors and millions of other readers, for literature sets us out as solitary and knits us together as a community.

OVERCOMING CHILDHOOD

Dorothy Allison's *Bastard Out of Carolina*

Amy Crawford

T HE SECOND YEAR I taught Women's Literature, a senior elective that attracts an eclectic mix of students—mostly girls—I started with *Bastard Out of Carolina*. But before I shared the title with my class, I offered this caveat.

> I've decided to start this year with a very challenging book. I don't expect you to have trouble with the vocabulary, nor will we spend all of our time tearing the book apart looking for symbolism. But for many of you, this book will be the hardest you've ever read. It's one of the most devastating books I've ever read, but it also made me smile and laugh. It's fiction, but it's based on a true story. And it's one of my five favorite books of all time.

Their attention piqued, most students appeared excited to dive in. But others were skeptical, wondering if I had dipped into Berkeley High School's renowned bag of depressing novels and plays. As an educator, I considered my choice. *Bastard Out of Carolina* elucidates many issues in students' lives. It is also very personal, requiring intense engagement. Not only is it challenging for my students; it is also challenging for me as a teacher because it brings many "taboo" issues to the fore. But bolstered by a transcendent experience with the text in my twenties, I was determined to give my students a chance to respond in a similar spirit.

As one among a dozen senior English electives, Women's Literature tends to attract students drawn to books by women, but not everyone fits that description. Students who are simultaneously taking AP Literature sit next to students scrambling to graduate on time. There are students of all backgrounds and ethnicities, who vary in their successes in school, and the flavor changes completely from one term to the next. During most semesters the students outnumber the desks, and yet only a handful of these students are boys. With this unusual mix of kids, reading *Bastard Out of Carolina* takes on a special meaning.

After giving each student a brand-new book and a starter set of sticky notes, I guided them through a ritual introduced to me by a college professor. "Okay, pick up the book in both hands and look it over. What do you look for when you choose a book to read? What do you look at when you pick up a book?" Someone said "the cover illustration," another "the title," another "the summary on the back," and yet another "reviews."

"So what are your first impressions?" I asked.

"It looks pretty good," LaShawn offered. "It's got a great title with a swear word in it and a female author with two first names, and the summary is interesting." A wave of noise washed over the room as students argued whether *bastard* qualifies as a swear word, but they found themselves agreeing that it made for an intriguing title.

"Plus it's a bestseller and won an award," added Alisa, an outgoing girl who lacked academic confidence. "People like it."

"Okay, now open the book. What's the first thing you see?" Many students kept flipping to the beginning of chapter 1, but I urged them to take it one page at a time, to enjoy the anticipation and pick up a few clues in the process. "Enjoy the physical book itself," I added. A few brought the brand-new books up to their noses and took a good whiff. Giggles and eye rolling followed.

"More reviews! I'm not reading those."

"Anything you can glean by looking them over, even if you don't plan on reading them?" I asked. Puzzled looks abounded. "Check to see who's writing the reviews. Sometimes you can pick up interesting information from those."

"Hey, Barbara Kingsolver wrote one. I've read some of her books," said Alisa.

"Me too," several classmates concurred.

"*Gay and Lesbian Times?* What's up with that?" asked Naima. Aha! Tension filled the air, if only for a moment. A sense of evaluation was palpable as the students sized up each other and me. Was that a homophobic question? Who was going to say something offensive? And what would I do? Most seemed to expect a class called Women's Literature to provide a respite from the hallways and other classrooms where kids and adults tolerate ongoing homophobic language; others hoped to find a place where they could say anything they wanted. I noticed a few furrowed brows.

Naima cut to the chase. "Is this about a lesbian?"

"Well, I don't want to give anything away," I began. A smile of satisfaction crossed the face of Alex, the openly gay boy in the front row who would talk to me a mile a minute before and after class but was silent when the room was full. "But I will tell you that the author is a lesbian, and she lives in California. Okay, turn the page, and what do you see?"

"The title page."

"That's right," I said. "Check it out. Any new information?"

"No, it's the same stuff that's on the cover."

"Okay, turn the page; what do you see?"

"Copyright stuff and a dedication."

"Okay, what is worth knowing from the copyright page?"

"Oh, I know!" cried Deandra, excited to join the conversation. Before the first day of school, all of my previous encounters with Deandra had been during my hall supervision period, when teachers have the pleasure of checking the passes of students they don't know, and Deandra was a regular truant during my shift. "When it was written! In 1993. No, 1992."

"Okay, and who wants to read the dedication?"

Deandra raised her hand and read aloud, "For Mama, Ruth Gibson Allison, 1935–1990."

"Oh, damn, that's sad," interjected Jamal. "Her mama died before the book came out." Heads bobbed in agreement.

"Okay, turn the page. I need another volunteer."

Alex smiled in recognition, raised his hand, and then read. "'People pay for what they do, and still more, for what they have allowed themselves to become. And they pay for it simply: by the lives they lead.' By Mr. James Baldwin." And we're off.

Told from the point of view of Bone, a prepubescent girl born Ruth Anne Boatwright who grew up in the 1950s in a poor southern family, this novel explores powerful themes—family, poverty, women's opportunities, religion, love, death, sexuality, friendship, violence, abuse, and molestation—that are relevant to teenagers poised to enter the adult world. As required reading in my Women's Literature course, *Bastard Out of Carolina* has been an especially effective tool in creating a classroom community, engaging nonreaders, and encouraging social activism and self-awareness while instilling empathy and understanding. Allison rivets her readers with exquisite storytelling, a poignant sense of humor, and a believable point of view. She relates her disturbing story in such a way that my young readers are transfixed—held to the page by a coming-of-age saga that aches with realism and truth. We read aloud until the bell rang, and I told students to finish chapter 2, attach sticky notes to key passages, and write down questions for the next day's discussion.

The following day students entered the room bursting with enthusiasm. They couldn't tell yet what this book was going to be about, but they knew that they were onto something they would enjoy. After outlining the ground rules for how we would conduct our discussion, I called on Vanessa, a self-proclaimed avid reader of women's literature, who started us off by asking, "What's going on with this family? On one hand they seem really close and like they care a lot about each other, but on the other hand they are crazy! Did you guys read about those uncles?" We collectively flipped to where Bone's uncles are introduced, and we followed as Vanessa read aloud. Her choice particularly thrilled me because these were among my favorite excerpts, perfect illustrations of the writing teacher's mantra, "Show, don't tell." I've used Allison's descriptions of the uncles, and of Uncle Earle in particular, every year as the basis for a character-sketch assignment. These passages, coupled with Annie Lamott's tips on writing about character in *Bird by Bird*, have, over the years, sharpened my appetite for people watching, and this is the first time that a student has pointed them out without my prompting. Vanessa began reading:

> Mama said he was called Black Earle for that black black hair that fell over his eyes in a great soft curl, but Aunt Raylene said it was for his black black heart. He was a good-looking man, soft-spoken and hardworking. He told Mama that all the girls loved him because he looked like Elvis Presley, only skinny and with muscles. In a way he did, but his face was etched with lines and sunburned a deep red-brown. The truth was he had none of Elvis Presley's baby-faced innocence; he had a devilish look and a body Aunt Alma swore was made for sex. (*Bastard Out of Carolina* [New York: Plume, published by the Penguin Group, March 1993], 24)

At that point agitated squeals and nervous laughter filled the overcrowded room. Even the boys responded to this description of Earle, a rough-and-tumble guy's guy who drinks away his pain and settles his differences with a good old-fashioned fistfight.

Vanessa read until she reached the last line before a break: "A man who really likes women always has a touch of magic." Scanning the room, I found many wrinkled brows and puzzled looks, as well as a few beaming faces.

Naima looked around the room, and then her hand shot into the air. "It's strange how a man who is such a loser—I mean he drinks, he fights, and he cheated on his wife—is being presented as kind of a good guy. How can you cheat on your wife and at the same time really like women? I don't get it."

"Yeah," chimed in Deandra. "She talks about how irresponsible they all are, how they're in and out of jail. How can she admire them?"

"But look at what she has to hold them up against," countered Liz, a slight girl who sat in the back of the room and rarely spoke. "Look at the women. Remember what Granny said about girls? That she favored her sons because they appreciated her while her daughters were selfish, full of themselves, and of no use to her. I wonder if Bone feels inferior because of her grandmother's sexist attitude."

"This is one messed-up family! You can tell it's real," shouted Jamal to a round of laughter.

Liz tried to bring the class back to her point. "It's kind of ironic that Granny favored her sons over her daughters considering Bone's description of her uncles. She calls them 'rambunctious teenagers' with no sense of responsibility or maturity. Meanwhile, the daughters are hardworking, taking care of themselves, their kids, and the men. In my opinion it was definitely the women who deserved all the praise."

"I just think it's sad that Bone feels limited by being a girl and wishes she was born a boy," said Yesenia. "I bet this was common in girls who lived in the South during that time." Across the room, heads bobbed in agreement.

A look of exasperation crossed the face of Nicole, a Louisiana transplant who moved to Berkeley several years ago. She liked it here, but she was continually surprised by her Berkeley peers' preconceived notions of other parts of the country. "I doubt it was just in the South," she said, her drawl just barely detectable. "And she's a tomboy."

"But back to Earle," said Vanessa. "Remember how much Daddy Glen looked up to him when they first went into the diner? So even though they're crazy and wild, they have a soft side, and people like them even though they're kinda scary. I think that's what the description is trying to get across."

As our first discussion of the Boatwright family wound down, students agreed that however wild and crazy these men are, Allison paints a realistic picture of how families can be. They recognized the Boatwrights' complexity—drunk, wild, and mean, but at the same time loving and tight-knit. They subject each other to insults and erratic behavior, but they are also willing to die to protect each other.

As our conversation drifted to the opportunities open to the Boatwright women, I noticed that more than half the class had contributed to the discussion so far. I made a mental note to remember who was yet to be heard from.

~

Up to that point, I was encouraged by the class's response to *Bastard*: abundant student participation, obvious interest, and relevant and intelligent conversation about the text; but I knew that the going would get tougher when we reached the difficult parts. In fact, this book's complexity, its subject matter, and the very taboos that were mentioned and brought into the discussion were among my main purposes for working with this novel.

Perhaps one of the greatest triumphs of Allison's novel is her ability to communicate bleak subject matter through the compelling, disarmingly honest voice of Bone. It is Bone's voice that carries readers through the novel, and it is her voice, I'm sure, that allows us to relate to her, to see that no matter how terrible her fate, she has the ability to persevere. Since she is a young girl, my class of primarily young girls feel an instant kinship with her. Her story allowed them to gain clarity on their own family relationships, and perhaps even appreciate them more. For the boys, Bone offers insight into a different reality within which the girls and women in their lives dwell simply by virtue of their gender. While a male perspective pervades the world we live in—television, history, the very foundations of our culture—and girls naturally pick it up by osmosis, seeing things from a girl's point of view is a rare experience for boys. But they all have experienced the simultaneous wonder, intrigue, and powerlessness of childhood, and Bone provides a compelling peek into a childhood that is universal yet different.

My Women's Literature class struggled like warriors through each difficult issue raised by *Bastard*—attacking the characters' flaws while examining the class's reflections on society's mores. Our first encounter with violence arrived at the hands of the Boatwright men, namely Bone's uncles. At first outraged by what they perceived as crazy male behavior, my students abandoned their otherwise politically correct, Californian vocabulary.

"They're a bunch of crazy rednecks," declared Naima.

"Stereotypical hicks," chimed in Alisa. "White trash."

While most students seemed willing enough to laugh, Vanessa didn't let this comment slide. "I think we should be careful about labeling people. Remember how early on we find out how much Anney hates that word *trash*?" We flipped back to the beginning of the book, and she read aloud: "Mama hated to be called trash, hated the memory of every day she'd ever spent bent over other people's peanuts and strawberry plants while they stood tall and looked at her like she was a rock on the ground" (3).

As the words sank in, one student pondered aloud Anney's bleak reality, and another reflected on her own family's indignation at not being able to make enough money in the "land of opportunity." The reappropriation of language came up, with some students arguing that you had the right to use a word that's been used against your people. Others asserted that if one person could use it, anyone could, and others maintained that no one had the right to use a slur.

At the book's first example of violence, students disagreed about how seriously to take the Boatwrights' schoolyard-style bullying. Some argued that however "ignorant" their violence may be, it was less menacing than the quiet rage building up inside Daddy Glen, a black sheep whose lifetime's worth of slights makes him frightening.

"Uncle Earle is saying how Daddy Glen should have defended his family when he bad-mouthed them, and instead all he did was smile," began Alisa. " 'If they had traded a few punches over it, bled on each other a little, and made up after, the whole thing would have felt better to Earle all around' [38]. It's like instead of talking about things, the Boatwrights just have a fistfight. It sounds crazy, but it never seems to get as serious," she concluded, sounding less than convinced by her own insight.

"No doubt," Yesenia concurred. "And Glen just lets things build up inside. Remember how early on it said Glen would kill anyone who touched Anney? What's gonna happen when he snaps?"

When Daddy Glen first transgressed the father/child relationship, students were convincing in their shock and outrage. That day's discussion began before the bell rang. Students were bunched up in small groups, checking in to make sure they read the passage right.

"I can't believe he molested her," began Yesenia. "It's so scary, especially because even in the telling she sounds so innocent."

"Yeah, why was he smiling when he was doing it?" asked Deandra. "That's sick!"

"This book hella reminds me of a movie I saw called *Once Were Warriors*," said Naima. "Both Daddy Glen and the dad from that movie have so much power over their wife and kids. Daddy Glen just decides that they're leaving, and that's what happens. In the movie the dad took his family away from his wife's family so that he wouldn't feel so inferior to them. Is that what Daddy Glen is doing? Is he intimidated by the Boatwrights' closeness?" Naima has tapped into what is referred to in battered-women's shelters as the "tension-building stage," in which by exerting control, the abuser begins to alienate his victim from her support systems, usually friends and family. Mei, a bubbly girl who had become really serious when we started reading this book and who had stayed silent until then, directed us to a passage that illustrates this principle:

> "Your Granny is the worst kind of liar. That old woman wouldn't tell the truth if she knew it." He put his hand under my chin, his big blunt fingers pressing once lightly and then pulling away. "You stay clear of that old woman. I'll tell you what's true. You're mine now. You and Reese just keep your distance from her." (52)

As the students struggled to understand Daddy Glen's motives, they agreed on one thing. "He has 'issues,' " Alisa explained. "He wants to have a family with his last name, with his family line, and since Anney now can't have any more children, he is going to adopt Reese and Bone and try to make them his own. He is already trying to force them to cut ties with the Boatwrights, which explains why he moved them all away, farther from their family."

Naima added, "Abusive men are full of male pride, and they don't want help from anyone else. It's like they feel they need to prove their masculinity to their wives and families when really their family couldn't care less."

As we progressed with the novel, students became increasingly concerned about Anney's role in protecting her daughter from her husband and argued over whether she was living up to her motherly responsibilities. Naima asserted that Anney, a fiery and strong woman, may have been "losing track of her power," and then read:

> When he let me go, there was a bruise and Mama saw it right away.
>
> "Glen, you don't know your own strength!"
>
> "No." He was calmer now. "Guess I don't. But Bone knows I'd never mean to hurt her. Bone knows I love her. Goddammit. You know how I love you all, Anney." (70)

After an uncomfortable moment of silence, Naima jumped back in. "It's crazy how he could take his anger and frustration out on a nine-year-old girl who doesn't even understand what's going on. And he did that right in front of Anney, and she barely got mad. She stands by him and every decision he makes for the family. It shows she is powerless in their relationship."

"Did you guys notice how Daddy Glen was calmer after he hurt Bone?" asked Yesenia.

"Yeah, that's totally creepy," said Vanessa.

"That's the way he releases stress. I usually take a long bath or exercise. Not hurt little kids!" said Yesenia.

"Plus, he always excuses everything by reassuring Anney that he loves all of them," said Alex.

"How can she believe him? Why doesn't she just kick him out?" asked Jamal.

I noticed that students were squirming in their seats and realized it was time to give everyone a chance to reflect on what was going on in the novel. I asked them to take a few minutes to write down their thoughts and feelings about the violence in the book. Their topics ranged from their frustration with Anney, to what they'd have liked to do to Daddy Glen, to how they wanted to save Bone, and to how they personally had been affected by abuse. They saw Daddy Glen as a ticking time bomb and couldn't understand how Anney, whom they perceived as powerful, would not recognize the danger she was bringing upon her daughters and herself by staying with him. For homework I asked students to search the library or Internet for information about the "cycle of abuse" and to be prepared to talk about it in light of that day's reading.

The following day students shared their informal research in small groups, and we charted out the patterns they had found on a wheel on the whiteboard. Together, we identified where and how the different stages—tension building, abuse, and remorse—had appeared in the text so far. As we moved on to the latest reading, Jamal questioned the way Anney got money to feed her family. When LaShawn suggested prostitution, Deandra cried, "What are you talking about? Where did you read that?"

"Didn't you notice? She put on all that makeup and dressed up. Where do you think she got the money?" needled Alex.

Allison stays true to the naïveté of childhood, and at times her narrative requires readers to read between the lines. Bone tells what she sees, thinks, hears, and feels, but it takes a reader's life experience to fill in the picture. Alisa commented on this technique, and we thought back to the other passages in which we'd encountered the same ambiguity.

The next day we were back to discussing Anney's mothering.

"Do you guys think she'll stay with Daddy Glen even though he beat Bone?" Yesenia asked the class.

Liz tentatively answered with a question of her own, "What else can she do?"

"She can leave," Jamal said confidently. "That's why my cousin don't live with his daddy."

"She could go live with one of her brothers or sisters," responded Alex.

"Maybe Daddy Glen threatens their lives," interjected Vanessa. "Maybe he says that he will kill her kids."

"I just want to know how much Anney will take before she leaves Daddy Glen," said Alisa. "Bone's had two broken collarbones and a broken tailbone. What's it gonna take?"

"Does anyone else think it's strange that Anney doesn't tell her family about this?" asked Nicole.

"Well, from what we've learned about abuse, it seems like she wouldn't tell her family," responded Vanessa.

. "I don't get it," continued Nicole. "Bone had a chance to tell the doctor, but instead she wanted to get home to be protected by her mother. How could she trust her mother to protect her at this point?"

"In many cases of child abuse," explained Vanessa, "the child feels as if she is in the wrong. It's like she has no self-esteem, and she feels she's not worth anything."

"It still doesn't make any sense to me," Nicole remarked adamantly. "I mean, at a minimum, Anney's brothers could kick some sense into him."

"You know," said Mei, voicing an opinion for the first time, "it's a lot easier to say that if you're not in the situation yourself. We can say what we would do all we want, but until it's happening to you, you don't really know what you'd do." Heads bobbed in agreement, and there was a moment of quiet, soon broken by Nicole.

"I still say it's crazy that no one's talking. Especially Anney."

⁓

The next day Naima brought up a topic that was on everyone's mind but that no one knew how to talk about. "What do you guys think of Bone's masturbating?" After a pause, she answered her own question. "I think this abuse is just too much for a ten-year-old, and it's not like she can tell anyone because *she* doesn't even understand it."

In high school, issues around sexuality are of intense interest to most students. Outrage about molestation and abuse comes up on an almost daily basis, but when the subject turns to sex, masturbation, and other "natural" acts, the students grow serious and mostly silent. Although a week later more students would join the masturbation discussion, for the time being, they were quiet.

Vanessa directed us to another passage showing the effect of the abuse on Bone's self-image.

> I knew it was nothing I had done that made him beat me. It was just me, the fact of my life, who I was in his eyes and mine. I was evil. Of course I was. I admitted it to myself, locked my fingers into fists, and shut my eyes to everything I did not understand. (110)

Naima was enraged. "God, this makes me so mad! Here is a grown man sexually abusing and beating a ten-year-old girl who doesn't even know about puberty yet. She's getting confused thoughts about sex, male-female relationships, fatherhood, and most of all about herself."

Yesenia jumped in. "It's like she thinks that since he's doing this, she must be doing something to cause it, but she's not. Ten-year-old kids don't know right from wrong. Whatever an adult does must be right."

From there a tangential conversation broke out about how important it is for adults, especially those with authority—as in a family or school or camp—to "act right," to set a positive example and create a safe environment for kids. I detected a shifting sense of self in some of my students, a few of whom, deep in the throes of wildness just last year, were awakening to their own power and responsibility in the adult world.

Alisa brought us back to the book by asking, "Do you guys think the abuse already made an irreversible impression on Bone?"

"Yeah, it's taken a toll on both her and Anney," said Naima.

"Bone is much less talkative now," continued Naima. "She's always reading, not talking to other people. And Anney looks all tired. She's lost her looks."

"They used to be so open with each other," added Yesenia, "but now it's like they can't communicate."

"I think Bone and Anney have different ways of dealing with it," said Liz. "Anney refuses to face reality. It's like she thinks that if she ignores it, it will go away. Bone just stores all the anger up inside. She escapes from reality by reading and listening to gospel and country music. But both of them are becoming secluded and quiet."

"I don't know," said Deandra. "She wrote this book, right? So she must come out okay." Deandra touched on a key misconception in reading literature with high school students—confusing the author with the narrator. And this fairly typical mistake was complicated because our experience of reading this book was in part shaped by our knowledge that something based on truth was being shared. Deandra's comment reminded me that we needed to talk more about narration, but it also suggested that a key reason my students developed such a profound relationship with this book—why they were compelled to engage respectfully, to identify with the narrator, and to believe this story—was that the story is true. Their experience mirrored my own experience of reading *Bastard* for the first time. Inadvertently, Deandra gave me some ideas to help students deal with the emotional fallout when they would finish the book.

As we moved to the second half of the novel, the students became increasingly empathetic to Bone and her battle for self-esteem. The hate and anger building up inside her alarmed them. They questioned her string of passing obsessions—attending revivals, listening to gospel music, and masturbating with a mountain-climbing hook she had dredged up from Aunt Raylene's riverbank. They worried about her deteriorating sense of self as they watched her make her way through a series of troubling events—observing the fiery death of her only friend, robbing a drugstore, experiencing the death of her beloved Aunt Ruth, and suffering another brutal beating at the hands of her stepfather. They watched her self-confidence dwindle as her dislike for herself and her surroundings grew. They wanted to save her from her solitude, her life, her living hell. They concocted solutions for her salvation: sending her off to live with an aunt or uncle, bringing her into their own homes. They worried about the violence that permeated her masturbation fantasies. They wished she had a confidante in Reese, her little sister. And through it all, more and more students joined in the conversation. Their respect for each other blossomed as their anticipation for classroom discussions and their willingness to share stories from their own lives grew. And at no time was this more apparent than on small-group discussion days.

On those days, randomly assigned groups huddled close together and talked in hushed tones about the book and how it connected with their lives. I circled the room and caught just enough of their conversations to know they were on topic. Occasionally a group invited me over to settle a disagreement or clarify a point, but most students were so deeply engrossed with each other that I almost felt like an intruder in my own classroom. Meanwhile, I thought about ways to parlay their interest in Bone's story into a willingness to grapple with difficult texts like *Woman Warrior* and *Beloved*.

Students arrived in class almost in celebration mode after reading how Aunt Raylene discovers evidence of Daddy Glen's abuse on Bone's body. But they continued to be troubled by Bone's attempt to keep the abuse a secret, even from the family.

"I don't understand why Bone didn't want Raylene finding out," began Nicole. "It seems like she should be happy that finally someone will protect her."

"Well, think about it," responded Liz. "She's drunk and must be scared to death that all these people are going to blame her for the beatings, just like Daddy Glen and Anney did. She still thinks the abuse is somehow her fault."

"She must have felt a lot of shame in letting the secret come out in the open," said LaShawn. "She's probably afraid Mama's gonna be mad at her for slipping up and letting everyone see her private shame. That must have been terrifying for her."

Putting themselves in Bone's shoes, students vocalized about the danger of blaming the victim. They saw the characters in the book with a complexity akin to that of the real people they knew; they saw bad situations that they were unable to fix, just like in real life. And they found power as the depth of their understanding of the book's events grew. Less mature readers want good guys and bad guys and expect a superhero ending in which the bad guys get their just deserts. But these young adults were coming to appreciate how literature has the ability to reflect the uncertainty and unevenness of their own lives. And while they celebrated the punishment the uncles unleash on Daddy Glen, their anticipation of it was tempered by Anney's response to being found out.

> I'm so ashamed I couldn't stop him, and then . . . I don't know . . . He loves her. He does. He loves us all. I don't know. I don't know. Oh god. Raylene, I love him. I know you'll hate me. Sometimes I hate myself, but I love him. I love him. (246)

"I hate her," snapped Deandra.

"I sure hope this gives Anney the courage to leave him," said Alisa. "It's time Anney acted like a mother and gave all of her attention to Bone."

"I'm sorry," said Alex, "but she is being a bad mother. She loves her kids, but she's putting them in danger by staying with Daddy Glen."

"I think she's being selfish," said Nicole. "Bone's being beaten because she is in love with Daddy Glen? HELLO! What kind of parent would do that?"

But living apart from Daddy Glen neither reestablishes the relationship between Bone and her mother nor alters Bone's belief that everything is her fault—that if she'd just acted differently, or been a different person, none of this would have happened. When Bone tells her mother she knows Anney's reconciliation with Glen is inevitable, Anney says, "I won't go back until I know you're gonna be safe," to which Bone replies, "I won't go back." After reading this exchange, my students became hopeful that Bone, however traumatized, has a good head on her shoulders and is becoming a strong young woman. They were appalled that a girl so young should be in a position to make such a decision, but they recognized her resilience and determination as traits that will help keep her safe and heal her wounds.

"The way she said so matter-of-factly that she was never going to cry again was so momentous!" said Liz. "It's like she's achieved some kind of peace, like she knows the worst is over."

"Or maybe she's become so strong and hardened that she feels Daddy Glen couldn't make her cry again even if he tried," said Naima.

"But what really makes me mad," retorted Deandra, "is that the only reason Anney leaves Daddy Glen is because her family finds out and her brothers kick the shit out of him."

"Hey, let's give her a chance," said Yesenia. "Maybe now that Bone has told her mom that she won't go back to Daddy Glen, Anney will stop considering it an option. Maybe she'll feel more responsibility to her ten-year-old daughter than to her abusive husband." Yesenia encouraged her classmates to consider how although Daddy Glen has never hurt Anney, by living with him and loving him she is so deeply drawn into the cycle of abuse that she too must be afforded space to make mistakes.

But that generosity of spirit is missing the next day when students returned to class devastated by the ending. We began class with a "quickwrite" in which students wrote down how they felt upon finishing the book. Deandra expressed what most of her classmates felt and needed to express before we could collectively grappled with the ending.

> I hate Daddy Daddy Glen so much, I hate him, I hate him I hate
> him. After reading this chapter I hurt inside, I felt pain tingle up
> my spine as I continued to read on and I tore the book. I hate
> her mama too. I hate that she is so weak. I hate that she is blind
> to him. I HATE HER. She is just as guilty by not doing anything.

Yesenia took Deandra's response one step further, examining the consequences of this ending for Bone:

> I almost cried when Bone saw the sheriff as Daddy Glen!! He was
> trying to help her. I hope she doesn't hate every man she meets
> from now on! More suicidal thoughts! And then she thinks no
> one cares about her! I can't even imagine feeling that alone.

Yesenia zeroed in on the possible lasting effects of the abuse, a point she would voice to the class, triggering a discussion about "being a 'victim'" and how survivors can overcome internalizing their "victimhood."

Alisa was horrified by the double betrayal, but she maintained that there is hope for Bone. She wrote:

> It's the ending of the book that has been the hardest part of the whole novel for me to grasp. There is no justification, no reconciliation. The only relieving thing about the end is that there seems to be a great shift in Bone's general disposition. She seems to empty herself of all that hate and rage, and in an unexplainable way, she is now pacified. She is humbled. There is also a sad trace that the cycle may continue, and that Bone has little determination to live her life differently than Anney's. Maybe she will live as Raylene does, and distance herself somewhat. And who knows what will become of her sexuality. In any case, she still has the rest of her family, which is more than I can say about Anney, and she will definitely continue the family legacy of a life of hardship. She is definitely a Boatwright. Even without a happy ending she still has strength and durability and a lifetime ahead of her to overcome the first 14 years.

Helping my students make sense of the book's ending took time and sensitivity. We began with a return to James Baldwin's epigraph, which elicited more questions than answers.

"Is this supposed to be a good thing or a bad thing?"

"Is this supposed to be about Glen or Anney?"

"Could it be about Bone, because some fool might say [that] by not telling she 'allowed' herself to be beaten?"

"But if the author is Bone, would she write something condemning herself?"

"But it doesn't necessarily condemn, does it?"

"Isn't it just another way of saying 'karma'?"

"What's karma?"

After extensive discussion, most of the class decided that Bald-

win's words, neither exclusively condemning nor celebratory, probably fitted all three characters. The epigraph allowed them to grapple
with forgiveness, hope, and self-determination, and they believed
that karma was on Bone's side.

To deepen their understanding of the novel, students began to
write. Some put their well-trained analytical essay skills to work and
explored the development of a theme, symbol, or character in the
novel. Others took a creative approach and wrote follow-up chapters, requiring them to think deeply about Allison's narrative style
and concluding their journey with the Boatwright family. I copied
these chapters for the entire class, and we read them together, offering
feedback to the authors. Others initiated a letter-writing campaign to
persuade Dorothy Allison to come and speak at Berkeley High School,
and to our delight, they were duly rewarded. Six months later she
spoke in a theater packed with students, some of whom had read
her work. As in the book, her stories of childhood made us laugh,
even as we struggled to hold back our tears. She responded to a boy's
question, an important question asked irreverently, with the utmost
sincerity and won over an uninitiated audience. In the week following her visit, many unfamiliar faces peeked through my window and
asked for a copy of "a book by that lady who read to us about her life."

∽

"One of the things I remember most about reading *Bastard Out of Carolina* was that we started the year with it, and suddenly girls who I'd
had classes with for years but who never said a thing were speaking up
in class." So began my recent conversation with Vanessa, now a college
junior who was home for spring break. "I also remember you warned
us about how emotionally difficult it was going to be before we began,"
she continued, "and then, while we were reading [it], feeling like for
the first time in school the entire class was being treated like adults."

Vanessa's words confirmed my suspicion that Allison's novel
helped transform this high school English class into a young adult
book group, prepared and eager to take on *Woman Warrior* and
Beloved. The book encouraged this and a handful of subsequent

classes—including students with few, if any, positive experiences with reading or with high school English under their belts—to interact personally and intellectually with an outstanding book. Through these discussions, new friendships were formed, friendships that broke down the ethnic, economic, and physical barriers that often segregate our students and obscure important values that schools strive to instill in our burgeoning adults.

Bastard Out of Carolina affected different students in different ways, some more obviously than others. Deandra visited me regularly the following semester asking for book recommendations "as good as Bastard Out of Carolina." Vanessa used the book as a way to try to make sense of the recent suicide of a loved one. Alex began a campaign to get approval for a Gay/Lesbian Writers English elective. Alisa gained confidence in her intellectual abilities and was a strong leader in our analysis of Beloved. Naima helped a friend extricate herself from an abusive relationship. Mei and Yesenia got involved with the domestic violence prevention group on campus. And many other students I have not named changed their thinking about a wide range of issues.

Bastard Out of Carolina inspired a shift of one sort or another in each individual, but what most impressed me was the students' collective relationship to the novel. When they filed into my room each day, I felt like the lucky host of a meeting of bright and hungry friends, impatient to talk to each other about this great book.

• CHILDHOOD STORIES •

• ABUSE AND RECOVERY •

CAN YOU FIND YOUR FUTURE IN YOUR PAST?

Toni Morrison's *Song of Solomon*

Dean Blase

I FIRST ENCOUNTERED
Song of Solomon at the age of nineteen, when it was presented to me
by a professor at the University of Michigan. In her course on narrative, we read novels that ranged in scope and quality from Fyodor
Dostoyevsky's *Crime and Punishment* to the trashy yet compelling
novels of Louis L'Amour and Barbara Cartland. *Song of Solomon* was
unquestionably the star of the show. It was a page-turner, a great read
that was satisfying in its craft and profound in its insights. Unlike the
equally compelling *Crime and Punishment, Solomon* offered me the
possibility of an adulthood suffused with magic and promise. In language that was breathtaking in its beauty and depth, it showed me
how to live purposefully.

When I began teaching, I was certain it would work well for the
students at my mostly white, suburban high school in the Midwest
who had read no works written later than *Catcher in the Rye*. I gave a
copy to the department head, hoping to see it added to our curriculum, but he nixed it, saying it was inappropriate (he had read only the
first chapter, in which Morrison hints at an incestuous relationship

between Milkman and his mother, Ruth—a relationship that is later explained in more reasonable terms by Ruth herself) and that "sometimes books need time to prove their weight—time will probably show this one won't be a classic." This was in 1993, more than fifteen years after its publication. Later that year, as it turned out, Morrison won the Nobel Prize for Literature, and I managed to contain myself, resisting the urge to give him a nice, hearty "I told you so."

Several years later, when I took over his American Literature classes, I piloted the book. I wanted a book for my students that didn't just present African Americans in their most downtrodden states, such as the required works by Maya Angelou, Frederick Douglass, and Mark Twain. I was sure that *Solomon*'s themes of finding one's identity, tracing a heritage that had come dangerously close to being obliterated, and the wisdom of its symbolic system would be a terrific personal and intellectual challenge for my students.

Since then, hundreds of my students have found their own ways through the novel, with a great range of responses. Johnny was fascinated with striking out from one's peer group; Rafael found the need to search for his heritage because of his adopted status; and Jesus discovered a potential way to heal our country's past of racial injustice and lack of redemption. Many students have been fascinated by the book's fusion of realistic details with fantastic flourishes (a technique reminiscent of Latin American literature's magical realism). This book is rich and powerful—in all the right ways. More than any other I teach, it has generated intellectual epiphanies and promises to "seize the day," and in one case it has even saved a life.

Flight opens Morrison's novel, with a suicidal madman bearing blue silk wings and an incomprehensible message to a field of spectators that includes a neatly dressed pregnant woman, a noble but ragged singer, an intelligent boy, and two young girls chasing after velvet rose petals. The opening scene is richly cinematic in its colors, drama, injustice, and death. It is also deeply confusing—Morrison catches us off guard, leading us to ask more questions than we can answer. I tell my students to be aware of this and to know that she is giving us half stories, pieces of truth that will shock and startle us—

perhaps even make us want to give up reading. But the book has a grander plan, and it offers a life lesson that my students learn along with the protagonist Macon Dead III, nicknamed Milkman.

In its simplest form, *Song of Solomon* is a familiar coming-of-age tale. Milkman is born into a family named Dead, which has more than its share of conflicts, and we follow the various threads of its members and their impact on his growing up. The opening chapter shows Milkman as a curious but underdeveloped young boy with a cruel father, also named Macon Dead, who is bent on creating financial success for himself; a mother, Ruth, who is startlingly overnurturing to her son; and two sisters with the unlikely names Corinthians and Magdalene Called Lena, who have scarcely any interior life but who cultivate doll-like exteriors. There are also a crazy drunken aunt named Pilate, and Guitar, Milkman's best friend, who is older, hip, and rebellious. We are continually fed new versions of each character's past and present through a series of shifting narratives that tell and retell pieces of the Dead family history until, after two-thirds of the way into the book, the family histories of the two generations finally fall into place. Milkman sets out to find gold but instead discovers his ancestors three and four generations removed. Along with this discovery comes the realization of a power that he holds—the ability to fly.

This self-awareness, which requires readers to believe in magic as much as they believe in the mythology of self-improvement that pervades the American bildungsroman, excites my students, sometimes even changing their lives. This is not, as it turns out, yet another novel that teaches them to follow the path of goodness so that they may live safely and solidly in the middle-class American Dream, or even one that counsels them to "believe in themselves," to become individuals transcending society's expectations and limitations. Rather, it is a book that discovers, through a long (and painful) process, that joy can be electric, and that discovering one's self in the past transcends mere self-knowledge—by experiencing your heritage, you can find who you really are—at the molecular, spiritual, and even magical level.

Although this book was the first of Oprah Winfrey's book club picks, Morrison's brilliance keeps this journey from becoming maudlin, sappy, or stereotypical. This—after a year of reading other American "heroes' journeys" in which the answer lies in Ben Franklin's list of thirteen virtues, in Huck Finn's unexamined West, in Gatsby's mansion and his long-lost "capacity for wonder," and in Holden Caulfield's never-ending carousel—comes as a relief to my students. And what, other than learning how to rediscover a severed heritage, can unite a nation of immigrants who have been torn from the physical and geographic connections to their multiple pasts, and who continue to desperately seek security by obsessively focusing on their present?

Invariably, students are confused at the beginning of the novel and need help sorting through the multiple and often contradictory stories that are told by the characters as Morrison slowly and skillfully builds the narrative of the Dead family and its associates. That stories need more than one teller to reveal their fuller truths is one of the strongest lessons my students learn—the idea that examining an issue from multiple sides and hearing the same story from multiple speakers yield a richer and more complete understanding. As students trace the emerging truths of the Dead family, I ask them to create a map of a story famous within their own families. How might a grandmother's version differ from a son's or father's? How can students, from their vantage point, weave the stories together to make sense of them themselves? We talked about multiple perspectives in the stories of our nation—McCarthy's take on communism, the views of labor workers, capitalists, and Arthur Miller, as laid out in *The Crucible*; more recently, the fallout from 9/11 as it appears from an Arab American perspective. One young woman, Grace, recognized her own growing ability (and her past culpability) to sort through cliquish gossip in the pages of *Song of Solomon*:

> In life, we learn about people primarily through what other people tell us. I'm told that high school is the time when each of us is labeled, and it's in college that we are created; that we make something of ourselves. I believe that comments like "she's a slut" or "he's an alcoholic" rarely result after frequent events, but instead after just one or two. Those statements are usually ex-

aggerations of the truth, and tend to result in a name that a person has to live up to. Like in high school, *Song of Solomon* has this recurring theme of misconception. Each character is misread, mainly because of a lack of a story.

Certainly the pain of having stereotypes assigned to her helped Grace be more patient when reading such seemingly strange tales about Pilate's being a snake, Ruth's being perverse, and Macon II's being a monster. When reading this book, students learn to avoid making snap decisions when they hear a story—to hold out for more versions, and even to seek out multiple perspectives for themselves. No longer do I have to battle the classic student assumption that there is a single "right" way to read a book. They discover for themselves the value of discovering multiple, valid approaches to reading texts and to understanding the world. This sort of understanding makes up a large part of what Milkman discovers, and seventeen-year olds, ripe for lessons in maturity, learn right along with him.

Seated at tables with large pieces of butcher paper and Magic Markers, students create linear narrative maps and see that Milkman's "adolescence" in fact stretches out much farther than his teen years: his dependence on his parents, his refusal to empathize with others, and, notably, his inability to love and be loved in meaningful ways don't end until his midthirties. For my students, the possibility of remaining stuck in adolescence loomed as a threat to their own independence, their own ability to move away from home and identify who they are, and their reliance on a worldview supplied to them only by their parents and by media sources bent on marketing to adolescents. Libby, a young woman who is one of a set of triplets, perhaps feels the need to individuate more than the average teenager. Consciously breaking down race and community barriers, she connected Milkman's eventual freedom with her own need to learn how to find more to life than the rigid expectations of her culture:

> Normally a sixteen-year-old suburban upper-middle-class white girl might not be able to relate to the black small-town character of Milkman. Because of another story, I can. J. R. R.

Tolkien wrote, "If more of us valued food and cheer and song above hoarded gold, it would be a merrier world," and it is through this that I can understand Milkman's journey in *Song of Solomon*. Milkman was on a search for two things: his identity and Pilate's gold. It really wasn't his idea to find Pilate's gold; in fact, he didn't even know if it really existed, but [only] through stories from his father. Like Milkman, I am on a journey to find my identity on this road we call adolescence. While on this journey I am mandated to obtain one thing: a good education. Forget about happiness; this is the age of opportunity ... opportunity that stems from good grades and a fabulous college education. In school we are condemned to the same daily routine in the constant pursuit of that gold star on our papers. But does it really matter? In the real world if you can't be yourself and tell what you think, who is going to care about how many gold stars you got in school?

Students like Libby want to move into the adult space that Milkman finally moves into and begin to find ways to do so throughout the book. The words of her parents and teachers echo through her response as traditional modes of "opportunity" become oppressive to her, keeping her from being herself and finding her own voice.

Once students have followed Milkman through his journey, in reading the final powerful words, "For he had learned ... that if you surrendered to the air, you could ride it," they are typically filled with exhilaration, questions, and the need to talk. They tumble into the classroom filling the air with their curiosity. "What did Guitar do?" "Where will he go?" "What about Pilate?" "Can Macon fly too?" "Why does Morrison pick flying?" "How come *ride* is italicized?" To help them make sense of this enigmatic ending, I direct them to reread the opening paragraphs of the book. The scene that had once stood in the way of their getting absorbed in the novel now provides answers from Morrison herself. The suicidal man in blue wings atop a building sharpens into focus as one of the Days, Guitar's group of revenge-seeking radicals. His blue satin wings become a costume worthy of a superhero trying to save the world. His occupation, a life insurance agent, makes sense as he promises to ensure a better future by seeking his own death. Even the name of the building—Mercy Hospital—provides magic for my students. Perhaps this man's "leap into the air," like Milkman, will offer release instead of madness. The crowd assembled below now has a context. Ruth is the woman in neat blue, pregnant with Milkman, whose birth is preceded by death. Pilate is the singer, uniting the paradoxical death/flight with the birth through the song that we now know leads to the title "O Sugarman done fly away / Sugarman done gone / Sugarman cut across the sky / Sugarman gone home." Sugarman becomes Shalimar, which then reveals itself as Solomon, the ancestral pot of gold that Milkman has discovered. Guitar is the young boy who foreshadows his strong sense of justice by correcting a white nurse, and Corinthians and Lena are the young women who scurry to collect velvet rose petals—symbols of their pampered and tragic lives, devoid of real passion. The keys to the entire novel, as it turns out, are there to be found in the opening pages. And allowing my students to find the answers empowers them to make further sense of the text on their own terms.

About halfway through the novel, we read Morrison's Nobel Prize acceptance speech. In it, she tells the tale of a blind, wise, old griot woman, rumored to be clairvoyant, who lives outside of town. One day, a group of young folks come to trick her, to test her powers by standing before her and saying that in their hands they hold a bird. They want her to tell them whether the bird is living or dead, making fun of her blindness. The wise woman is silent for a long time, but finally she answers, "I don't know whether the bird you are holding is dead or alive, but what I do know is that it is in your hands. It is in your hands." Morrison then takes this fable and plays with it as metaphor. She explores the idea that the bird might in fact represent language. That the children must learn from her whether the language they know might breathe or die. She then moves further, adapting the story so the young people who appear before the old woman are in fact not there to trick her but want to know in earnest whether the language they have inherited is already dead. The old woman embraces the young people, saying, "Finally . . . I trust you now. I trust you with the bird that is not in your hands because you have truly caught it. Look. How lovely it is, this thing we have done—together."

It is this optimism, this generosity of spirit, that invites my students to spend time with this book. Readers who take the time and accept the challenge of this book take with them a different story, a different meaning for themselves. This, of course, is one of the great thrills of reading, but rarely before, if ever, have my students experienced it in such partnership with an author.

~

I always finish this unit by asking my students to develop their own line of analysis, their own approach to finding an answer to the book's complexities. Although at this point in their junior year they typically have written a half dozen literary analyses, none is as rewarding as this one.

They start with journal responses in which they identify promising kernels that could grow into a fully realized analysis and then start talking with one another about how they might connect the various hunches they had sketched out in writing. Topics ranged from botanical imagery to violence and righteousness, to civil rights, to sexual passion, to the color red and the economics of fabric. Within these topics, students often find keys to themselves.

Scottie, a young woman with extraordinary sensitivity to others but whose altruistic outlook sometimes leaves her unable to attend to her own needs, found inspiration in the strong character of Pilate. At first, I didn't see where her response was headed but then found her connections toward the end:

> Today, while reading *Song of Solomon*, I heard what could only be thunder. Then I heard the magnificent sound of rain falling in sheets upon the ground outside my window. As soon as I was able to pull myself away from the sound, I bolted up-

stairs and out the kitchen door and down the driveway. I couldn't contain my jubilation, and began jumping and flailing like a small child until I slipped in a particularly muddy spot.

I have loved mud as long as I can remember. Up until I was in grade school my family would go down to the Ohio River for vacations or just weekends. I remember the squishy mud between my toes and the clay banks that became better slides than anything manufactured. The best mud memory I have is from a particular day when my grandma, my sister, and I all painted our faces with different colors of mud. They were both clowns, and I was a tiger, wild and muddy.

When I slipped on the mud in the driveway, and felt the gritty yet smooth substance, I remembered that self-proclaimed tiger from before. I had a burning urge to reimmerse myself in the mud I obviously belonged in. At seventeen I was having one of my "moments." That's when I thought of Pilate, who lives life as one big moment. While every other character has these same raw emotions, yet cannot deal with them, Pilate has self. She doesn't lead the double life almost every other character goes through. Pilate is a strong and rounded personality full of woman developed by years. Her lack of a navel suggests a lack of influence on her by others.

For me, *Song of Solomon* is about a basic urge to seek out one life, one way in which to be content, and live it. Why do I live my life going through monotonous rhythms every day? That muddy tiger is what I become in my moments. Can't I live my entire life as the girl I want to be instead of leading two lives with the sole purpose of driving myself mad?

In Pilate Scottie discovered a model for seizing the day, which resonated much more strongly with her than did Emerson's weighty prose or Thoreau's lengthy descriptions of Walden Pond. I love the fact that the tiger who emerges from her childhood can inform her vision of adulthood.

Another vision of freedom and adulthood came from Marian, who for several years had been caring for her terminally ill mother. Through *Song of Solomon*, she seemed to have found the potential to fly off on her own, discovering that like Milkman, this desire had been with her ever since she could remember.

> I used to try to catch birds, but never could. I used to try to be like them by flying, but never could. As I grew older I no longer thought they were beautiful creatures, but rather I thought they were disgusting, disease-carrying animals. However, I realize now that it is not the animal itself that I was so enthralled with and later feared, but rather what they symbolized to me, which was freedom.
>
> I dreamed of being able to soar on my own, but as I come closer to being able to fly off into the sunset without my parents standing by my side, it seems harder than ever. As Milkman grew up, he still lived with his parents. He wanted to fly and get away from anything that was holding him back, like his mom and dad and even his name. As a grown man he seemed less concerned with flying; however, the reader knows that one day we will get a chance to fly because of all the bird imagery in the book which acts as a reminder to Milkman and to the reader not to give up on dreams, especially the dream to fly.
>
> Milkman went on a journey, and although he learned a lot, the main thing he learned was that it is possible to fly. Though I physically can't fly, I know that one day, I will be free to fly off on my own like Milkman. After all, "If you surrendered to the air, you [can] ride it." (*Song of Solomon* [New York: New American Library, Signet edition, 1978], 337)

Looking at her immediate future of caring for her mother when her peers were going to college, Marian's feelings about what it means to fly and be "free" in the traditional teenager sense (moving away from home and starting a new life) were full of conflict for her.

It was with Louisa, however, that I first understood the life-changing power of this book. I had taught Louisa in both seventh and ninth grades, and knew her to be a young woman who was bright and intelligent and who set high standards of perfection for herself. When she appeared in my junior American Literature class, I immediately knew that something had gone seriously wrong. Her hair was dull, her eyes were too bright, and her bones stuck out alarmingly. She pointedly drank water during class and ate nothing but rice cakes in our first period. During an out-of-class meeting at which lunch was to be served, I watched her take out a packed lunch and play with the food in an attempt to fool us into thinking that she was eating. These are all warning signs to those of us who teach middle-class suburban girls, and I was alarmed and saddened to see Louisa apparently succumbing to anorexia. As is our usual procedure, I immediately contacted the school nurse to see whether the family was concerned or had noticed the weight loss. The nurse assured me that Louisa had recently had back surgery and had been advised to keep her weight down to minimize her pain during her recovery. I touched base with Louisa's mother, who told me the same story. I kept an eye on Louisa, hoping to see a return to health. When several months had gone by and her condition seemed to be worsening, I decided to talk with her directly.

We met in the writing center, and I expressed my concerns about her health and appearance. Louisa thanked me for noticing but assured me that she had it "under control" and that she and her mother had recently decided to go on diets together—Louisa would eat more protein, and her mother would eat less food. Something didn't seem right, however, for as we continued to talk, Louisa told me that her parents had had problems and that she was having a hard time adjusting to the changes. She brightened at the end, trying again to give a convincing show that "everything was all right," and we ended our conversation with a hug and her again thanking me for taking an interest in her. I reported our conversation to the school nurse, who again assured me that the doctors wanted Louisa to keep her weight down to hasten the healing of her back. I couldn't shake off the feeling that Louisa was in danger. As painful as it was to admit it, I knew that my role had ended there. I wanted her to get better but knew that ultimately her health was in her doctor's hands. The nurse had suggested to her mother that she obtain counseling for Louisa, and as far as I knew, Louisa was receiving it.

At the end of the year, when students had finished reading *Song of Solomon* and Louisa had chosen her essay topic, I knew that my concerns about her eating were well founded. She chose to write about nutrition in the novel. There are several scenes in which characters cannot provide nutrition to others, cook meals perfectly, or else offer nutrients in ways that are complex—resulting in empowerment for some but not for others. Louisa traced these various scenes and identified them as being central to the book's message of empowerment. Food, control, and power are large issues in anorexia. I again touched base with the nurse and her mother, and again was assured that everything was fine.

It was not until I saw Louisa the next year, however, that I learned the story from her perspective (an essential Morrison message). She returned to school as a senior looking noticeably healthier, with color in her face and shine in her hair. She was relaxed and happy in a way I had not seen her since her freshman year. When I caught up with her and had a chance to talk about her regained health, what she said surprised me. She immediately connected her ability to control her weight and her life to having read *Song of Solomon*. I asked her whether her paper on the book had anything to do with her own issues about food, and she said that it did.

> The book really hit home for me; when you read it, you find something within yourself and you can go with it. At the time I read that book, I was at an all-time low. I couldn't control anything, and by reading *Song of Solomon* I found myself and found out who I was. Milkman's flying helped me see that you make your own wings. Everything I had to do to get healthy and to make my family work for myself could come from inside. The

wings sprout outward from within—you build the foundation for it based on who you are. I knew I had health inside of me— Pilate showed me that—and I realized that the shell of myself had gotten away from that.

I was astounded. I had, after all, seen the physical transformation—a descent close to the kind of anorexia that cannot be turned around. I asked her what her therapist had said about all of this, assuming that she had gone to one. She told me that other than a group therapy session about her parents' problems, she had received no counseling about her health. I asked her if anything else might have contributed to her change, and she answered thoughtfully, "I honestly don't think anything else could have pulled me out of it—something dangerous and big would have had to have happened."

When I asked her how she thought a novel could have such a profound effect, she answered, "That month it started with the book. I was looking up stuff on food and researching, and then, eventually, it hit me that it was me writing about myself, not her [Morrison]—I used her to get to me." I asked her about other books that she had read for school and what she had enjoyed. She thought through her reading lists over the past few years and recollected the amazing language in Zora Neale Hurston's *Their Eyes Were Watching God* and the raw voice of Holden in *Catcher in the Rye*. She reported loving the language in Joseph Conrad's *Heart of Darkness*, becoming captivated by his travels down the river, saying, "He had to reflect on himself and figure himself out, and we do too." Returning to *Song of Solomon*, she noted, "Kids who are juniors and seniors are trying to figure out who they are—they're about to go off on their own, and we need to be able to be ourselves first, because your group of friends won't be there." She liked the back rub that Milkman eventually gives and receives from a generous girlfriend. She loved the moment at which Milkman discovers his deep connection to his heritage; sitting at the base of a tree, "he grew his own roots, and grows up after that." She loved the final flying scene, finding it amazing that anyone could construe it as anything but flying (some of her more cynical classmates had thought he purposely jumps to his death), and found strength in a scene where Milkman walks through a large crowd in which everyone is moving in the opposite direction, noting that "he's going against the ebb of the tide, but I know what I have to do—it's the beginning of his discovery of who he wants to be."

That a year later Louisa could have such precise memories of this book, which by her own admission had pulled her out of an anorexic state and allowed her to discover her adult self, cheered me up. In fact, many of the students that I interviewed for this chapter immediately put their fingers on specific moments in and recollections of the book. *Song of Solomon* is memorable and important. It works to heal and to inspire. It teaches lessons that soft-focus posters in guidance offices try to get across with kittens and rainbows, but without ever veering into cheesiness. Morrison's wisdom is at its most accessible here—I can't imagine teaching without it.

• LEGACIES: THE IDENTITIES WE INHERIT FROM THE PAST •

• THE POLITICAL STRUGGLE FOR FREEDOM •

HOW DANGEROUS CAN A BOOK BE?

Mark Twain's *The Adventures of Huckleberry Finn*

Emily Donaldson

Notice: PERSONS ATTEMPTING to find a motive in this narrative will be prosecuted; persons attempting to find a moral in it will be banished; persons attempting to find a plot in it will be shot.
BY ORDER OF THE AUTHOR
—*The opening of Mark Twain's*
The Adventures of Huckleberry Finn

HERE ON CAPE COD, far removed from the concerns of a teacher's Sunday afternoon, I have to ask myself whether the warning at the beginning of *The Adventures of Huckleberry Finn* is actually a prediction, and a prescient one at that. To be sure, my students and I escaped from our collective journey with *Huck Finn* without being prosecuted, and no one was shot. But have I in a way been banished for "attempting to find a moral" in *Huck Finn*, for disturbing with the prodding stick of academic inquiry the shadowy waters of established race relations? If I had known how much trouble it would be to read this book with my students, would I have tackled it? More important, would I make the choice to read it again?

～

The custom at my school, a large urban high school in a university city, was for teachers to write their own curricula, so I curled up with a pile of books during my summer "off" to plan my eleventh-grade Advanced Placement American Literature course. Although my African American Studies background would heavily influence the whole course, I wanted to write one unit specifically geared toward thinking about race and racism. As I began, I realized with some dismay that I had never read *Huckleberry Finn*. I could not even remember hearing it mentioned in a class, not in my childhood years as a student in that same city's progressive public schools, not in college. I read *The Adventures of Huckleberry Finn* in one or two sittings and started over again as soon as I had finished.

～

My class had a considerably larger portion of white students than any class I had taught in my previous two years. One-third of the students at the school are white, but my AP class was four-fifths white. This class lacked a "critical mass" of students of color, but I did not want to shy away from conversations about race and racism.

Such conversations, and units such as the one I wrote for this course, Race and Racism in American Literature, should not be designed to prop children's eyelids open, to force them to stare at as much horror as possible. My own childhood education suffered from excessive horror, seemingly for its own sake. In third grade, my class studied the dropping of the bomb on Hiroshima. Each subsequent year comprised a gallery of horrors: the holocaust, slavery, conquest of the Western Hemisphere and Africa, Japanese internment, etcetera. But the lessons of this litany were unclear. As a teacher, I want to help my students see how the issues in *Huck Finn*, the problems Malcolm X identifies, the historic tensions in our literature, appear on our televisions every day. Racism is not something from "back then" or "the olden days," as my younger students say. Too many of my students don't believe in racism, or even racial stereotypes, viewing them instead as part of a mythic history that may or may not have actually occurred.

On the other hand, before I wrote *Huck Finn* into my indelible plan for the year, I asked an experienced colleague who had been my favorite teacher and was now my mentor what she thought of the choice. She told me it was a difficult book, that she had stopped teaching it when confronted with the pain it raised. She said she hadn't felt quite well versed enough in talking through issues related to race to teach it again. But she didn't tell me not to teach it, either.

$\sim$

By the time we were ready to start *The Adventures of Huckleberry Finn*, we had already been talking about race and racism in literature and in our lives for four weeks, but I begrudgingly acknowledged the flutter in my stomach the day I assigned the first freewrite that would prepare us for *Huck Finn*. I felt strongly that I could not require my students to start reading the book without a warning of the language and content. To be direct: I did not feel that I could, in good conscience, require them to read the word *nigger* in assaultive repetition without discussion and preparation.

My students varied widely regarding their ideas about race. Earlier, some of my white students had vehemently argued that if a text was written during what they called a racist time, the text itself could not be considered racist. Many white students seemed to view racism as a thing of the past, whereas students of color, African American students in particular, wrote about the persistence of racism. We had talked about the social construction of race and its genetic insignificance. We had discussed Malcolm X's idea of "kindly condescension." Through our readings, we debunked the idea that racism is simply individual prejudice or "acts of meanness," which encouraged my students to understand racism as a larger system of oppression.

Still, I assigned the freewrite with some trepidation. I wrote the assignment carefully on the board: "Freewrite on the 'n' word. How has this word been used in our history? How is it used now and by whom? How does hearing/using this word make you feel? Should we use it or read it in the classroom? Does the racial composition of our class affect whether we should use or allow this word?"

Every single one of my students turned the freewrite in, and they had written twice as much as usual. The weight of the stack in my hand betrayed its emotional contents. They were breathlessly impassioned. Monique, one of the few African American girls in the class, wrote that her parents had taught her never to say the word, but that she did not protest when her black friends used it. Brian wrote that he hated the fact that black kids could say it when he couldn't, that he was tired of being oppressed because he was white and a boy. Miguel explained that mostly his African American friends used it, but he usually did not, feeling that as a Latino he wasn't entitled to do so. Elizabeth described her discomfort about the topic and suggested I ask the African American kids whether we should use the word in our classroom. Many students reported that the usage of the word had shifted. Ronnie claimed it, emphasizing the difference between the spelling and pronunciation of *nigger* and *nigga*. Some white students asserted that no white people ever used the word anymore.

～

When we discussed the freewrites in class, the same mix of ideas, confusion, and anger emerged. Joe said, "I have a friend who works and hangs out with almost all black kids, and he would never say that word under any circumstances; his friends even make fun of him for it. He feels it's just wrong for white people to use it, ever." As he finished speaking, Joe shook his head a bit and looked at his sneakers.

"I agree with Joe that it's wrong for white people to use it," Elizabeth started, her usual enthusiasm somewhat muted. "But it is confusing when, um, African Americans use it with each other. I'm not saying it's wrong or whatever, it's just weird."

Daniel was next. He often spoke with an authority that I knew struck some of his classmates as arrogant. "Well, I think it's a form of power. I think black kids use it to have power over white kids. And it works. I mean, look, I'll just be honest here. I'm on the basketball team, and most of the other guys on the team are black, and they use it with each other. And when they do, I feel left out. They have a bond, a connection, that I am not part of."

I was pleased that he had revealed this in a sensitive and genuine way.

Ronnie looked at me urgently. "Can I say something?" he asked. I assented, letting him move up in the speaking order. "Daniel, now you know how it feels to be black most of the time. I mean, there's all kind of things that we're left out of, know what I mean?"

Daniel looked at Ronnie. I remembered with discomfort that Daniel had written in a freewrite that he had never realized that African Americans could be his intellectual equals until recently, until he met Ronnie in particular. "But Ronnie," Daniel asked directly, "do you think it's exerting a form of power or not?"

"Yeah, I do. And it's taking some of that power back that should belong to us."

Amy, a white girl, was next. She sat next to her close friend, Hannah, a biracial girl who wrote brilliant essays but hardly ever spoke in class. "But I think it's important that we remember that this is not always accepted as powerful. I mean, I know many black grandmothers and stuff who don't think this is good at all."

Monique shifted in her chair and looked down at the floor from behind her red glasses, which matched her shoelaces. "I would never say it front of my grandmother, I know that."

~

"I don't know about some of these kids, Emily man," Ronnie said when he dropped by my class after school with Miguel and Jeff. They formed a common trio in my class and outside of it.

"What do you mean?" I asked.

Ronnie began. "I mean, like Daniel saying that stuff about how he feels left out on the basketball team, like it's so terrible or something. He just doesn't get it."

"Did it offend you when he said that?" I asked.

"Yeah, kind of. I mean, know what I mean?"

"Yes, I think so," I said. "But I think Daniel was just saying how he feels, what his experience is with the word. I don't think he's trying to be offensive."

"But doesn't he understand that black people have to deal with so much of that, all the time, with being kept out and pushed down?" Ronnie persisted.

"No," I said simply, "he doesn't. All he can do at the moment is talk openly about his own experience. That's part of what this class is about, though—to raise everyone's awareness. We can help each other understand."

"But it's so hard," said Ronnie. "I mean, I can say all this stuff to you now, but how can I say it in class? With all them AP kids? And, like, Elizabeth and them. She's nice and everything, but she just looks at me like *I'm* supposed to tell her what black people think or something. It's weird." He scrunched up his face and then shook the expression off, looking at his friends. "Know what I mean?"

The other boys nodded together. They had talked about this before. "Well," I said, "it's not your responsibility to be, like, the black voice. How could you be anyway? But you should be able to express your views."

"I just stay quiet," Jeff said, quiet even then.

"Why?" I asked.

"Because. I feel like they're always . . . I feel self-conscious, like whatever I say is gonna be picked apart or something."

"How can I help you feel more comfortable speaking without making you feel like you have to represent millions of people?"

They looked right at me.

"I don't know," Jeff said.

"Well, can you think about it? It's important. And if you want me to talk to anyone in particular in the class, I would be happy to do that."

We talked for two hours. I was glad the boys felt comfortable enough to initiate contact with me and to talk so openly. *Well, the hardest conversation is over,* I thought.

~

It was as if a bell rang somewhere when the word "nigger" was spoken in my classroom. Not long after we began our preliminary conversations about *Huck Finn,* I was visited by an outside consultant who had been hired to work on race and diversity issues within our school. This person raised objections to my discussing the word "nigger" with my class, on the basis that a white teacher shouldn't talk about such things. Eager to foster dialogue and allow for criticism, I talked with this person at length. I thought I explained what my purposes and goals were in having such a difficult and potentially painful discussion.

While I was attempting to open up one kind of conversation, in which professional adults with similar goals collaborated to find a way to work productively on complex issues, another began in its place. I still don't quite understand what that other conversation, the one that took place beneath our words, consisted of, or how it became as contentious as it was to become.

~

So we started *Huck Finn.*

"Make sure you have your books out," I urged, surveying the students' preparations for the period. I took my seat, a blue rolling chair my younger students fought over. "First of all, let's talk about frames."

"Well, he frames it all with the Notice," Sage started.

Jimmy volunteered that the Notice was a warning to English teachers, those people who are always trying to invent meaning when there is none. "Good," I replied to his gentle jab. "Maybe he's warning intellectuals, the academy, teachers. What else?"

Other kids offered possibilities: that it was a dare, that it was a joke, that Twain was using reverse psychology to get us to think more deeply.

Monique raised her hand. "I don't know if this is a frame or not, but here it says the setting is 'forty or fifty years ago.'"

"That's a crucial frame, in fact," I said. "Twain finished writing the book in 1885, after the Civil War, after the end of Reconstruction. But the book is set in 1835–1845, according to him. So we have an antebellum setting but a post-Reconstruction context."

Mary said in her small voice, "He uses a first-person narrator to tell the story; he even has Huck say that Mark Twain is not writing the story. And Mark Twain's not even his real name anyway."

"Right! What is the effect of this?"

"It makes us believe it more."

"But it also distances Twain from it, like this is not Twain's story, but Huck's. Maybe Huck is responsible for it."

My kids rightly pointed out that lower-class Huck doesn't understand many of the customs that seem obvious to us. He doesn't understand that Tom Sawyer is just playing at being murderers and robbers. He says he prefers hell if Tom Sawyer is there too. He is hugely superstitious and believes in ghosts. He doesn't like wearing clothes or living indoors.

Katrina, a sensitive girl devoted to her faith as a Jehovah's Witness, said, "I think he's depressed." She pointed out Huck's lonesomeness, his abusive father. "He even wishes he was dead."

We discussed whether these qualities made Huck a reliable narrator and then moved on to Jim.

"Um, I think Jim's kind of stereotypical," Amy said hesitantly. "I mean, like the part where he brags about being ridden by a witch. He's so gullible."

"Let's read the passage," I suggested, "in which Huck describes Jim's reaction to the trick Tom and Huck play on him, and Jim tells the story of being ridden by a witch over and over again. Page four, at the bottom. It starts 'As soon as Tom was back.' "

Elizabeth volunteered, "I'll read." I thought I saw a cloud on her face as she scanned the paragraph. One, two, three . . . this is the paragraph with seven instances of "nigger" and "niggers" in twenty-seven lines. I remembered Jeff's freewrite, which expressed his feeling that having white classmates avoid the word was worse than hearing them use it. Seated at my left, he silently turned to the page. Elizabeth read carefully and exhaled when she was done. "That was really uncomfortable," she muttered, looking down, uncharacteristically shy.

"It's okay," I said. "It's okay to be uncomfortable about it. So the obvious question: why does this word appear seven times in this paragraph? What's the point of that?"

"It's so excessive, it's almost like he's making a point," Mary offered.

Amari, biracial and seemingly comfortable in many worlds, countered, "The point is that Jim's a fool, though. And so are all the other slaves who believe him. I mean, it's pretty straightforward."

"But maybe Twain is making the point that this word is heard so often that Huck is desensitized to it?" Rachel suggested.

Amari stretched his legs out under his desk and looked at Rachel. "I don't know," he said. "Sounds like you're reaching, as Emily would say."

Daniel piped up. "Wait a minute. We just said Huck is superstitious; Huck doesn't always know what's going on. So Jim is superstitious too. So what? Huck believes in witches; Jim believes in witches."

"I don't know, Emily," Tom said turning to me. "It seems like you spent all this time teaching us to recognize stereotypes, and now that we see them, you're trying to say they're not stereotypes." Tom, one of the white kids who had earlier written that racism was a thing of the past, had been particularly resistant to some of our discussions, and he seemed frustrated now.

"Well, Tom, I can't tell what I make of the depiction of Jim. In some ways, I see how Twain makes him subversive. We'll talk about many examples of Jim's strength and intelligence. But sometimes he's such a caricature, it's hard to see around it."

Jimmy said simply, "Jim's just making money, or whatever. He's telling this story, he gets all famous, the other people come to hear the story, and they even pay him money to hear it. Who says he even believes it? Seems smart to me."

~

In light of what my mentor had told me about teaching *Huck Finn* and what I knew about the treacherous territory of race, I had expected to encounter various difficulties while reading it. I expected to talk with students and their parents, perhaps at length, about the book and the feelings and issues it raises. What I did not expect, however, was what happened after my initial conversation with the consultant. Her initial objection about our "n"-word discussion quickly spread to one or two other people in the school community and turned to criticism about my teaching *Huck Finn* on the basis that the text was racist. I tried to explain that my class was seriously discussing the possibility of racism in the text. I pointed out the ways that *Huck Finn* advocates against racism.

But throughout my contact with adults, I was constantly frustrated that discussing the book itself proved impossible. For some reason, perhaps many reasons, they just wouldn't do it. So, the book became this odd territory for the adults involved in what was now an openly acrimonious discussion. On the one hand, it was the locus of all the trouble, the focal point of the objections raised. On the other hand, discussions allegedly about the book and what I was teaching quickly sped off onto other tracks. I wanted to talk about the book, but that seemed irrelevant to the people who objected. To them, it seemed, it was both all about the book and not about it at all. We never found a way to bridge that gap.

Meanwhile, my students talked with me for an hour at a time—and they continued their discussions outside of class for longer than that—about the book itself every day for weeks.

Each student was assigned a particular motif to track throughout our reading of *Huck Finn*. Every time ("Every *single* time, Emily?") a student's motif was mentioned, he or she had to record its appearance. Some of the recurring motifs were lonesomeness, superstition, the river, snakes, religion, and money. I assigned Rachel to work with snakes, knowing that from practicing Judaism she had some experience with the Bible.

"What's the point?" she asked bluntly, looking up at me from her desk.

"I don't know yet," I said. "I just know that snakes appear often in the text and generally carry symbolic significance."

"I don't think they're significant, but I'll do it."

I agreed, remembering that I had reported to her father at a conference, "I think Rachel is overcoming the idea that English class is all about people making things up." Her father had responded, "Isn't that what it is? People making things up?" So I wasn't surprised at Rachel's resistance, and I knew she would turn in first-rate work, even if she allowed that it was only an intellectual exercise.

In class, we were talking about chapters 8 through 10, in which Huck and Jim meet up and join forces on Jackson's Island.

"Okay, guys. The setting in these chapters is Edenic, like the Garden of Eden. We've heard that Huck's father looked like Adam, all covered in mud. Now Huck is alone on the island, or so he thinks, eating berries, living off the land, etcetera. Then a snake appears. Why does Twain put his characters here? What's up with this snake?"

Rachel raised her hand. "Well, I don't agree that it's Edenic, but a snake does lead Huck to Jim in a way. Huck chases the snake and comes upon Jim's fire."

Dylan, eager to get to the point, readily accepted my initial premise. "So, is Jim Eve here or what?"

Meredith, always attentive to textual details, said, "But remember later, in chapter ten, Huck brings a snake to Jim by putting the dead snake in his bed, and the snake's mate comes and bites him."

Dylan: "So Jim would be Adam, and Huck would be Eve, because it's Eve who brings the serpent to Adam by telling him to eat the fruit."

Meredith, book open: "Wait, I wasn't done. On page forty, the snake bites Jim on the heel, and that's one of the consequences for Eve in the Bible, that Eve will crush the snake's head and the snake will bite her heel."

Dylan, pushing back in his chair: "So Jim is Eve, then."

Rachel brightened, speaking as she raised her hand, "I have an idea. Maybe it's not simple like that, Dylan. Maybe it's not like Huck equals Eve or Jim equals Eve. It doesn't matter. Here, the snake brings Huck to Jim, like the serpent leads Eve and Adam to the tree of the knowledge of good and evil."

Dylan, joking now, "Ah! So Jim is the tree!"

"Stop it!" Rachel insisted. "No, but the serpent brings them together, leads them to the knowledge of good and evil, because they're probably going to learn about interracial friendships or something, and Huck is already changing his ideas about good and bad."

"That's a really good idea, Rachel!" I enthused. "You're onto something there."

Rachel instantly sulked back in her chair. "No, I'm not," she said. "It's bull—" she interrupted herself before the curse slipped out. "I was just making stuff up. Whatever."

~

Eventually, a decided struggle between me and the couple of people who objected to my use of *Huck Finn* emerged. News of the problem spread like wildfire throughout the community, or so it seemed to me as I declined interview requests from the local newspaper and resisted the urge to tell my story to anyone who would listen. Many teachers and administrators supported me. Colleagues of all colors came to tell me that they had heard about my predicament, that they supported me, and that they thought I was doing important work. Yet, I continued to feel dissatisfied with the conversations I had in countless meetings with various people. In the end, perhaps neither the conversation I wanted nor the conversation the other side wanted took place.

~

"Okay. So, today we're going to continue talking about the issue of the depiction of Jim. Is he a stereotypical antebellum 'happy darky' like we learned about in *Ethnic Notions,* or does he counteract this stereotype in some way? Or both?"

Mary said, "Um, I don't want to say this, but he still sometimes sounds kind of stupid to me, and I can't tell whether that's the dialect or how he really is."

"Yeah," Ronnie agreed, chin on top of crossed arms on his desk, puffy coat still on. "He sounds dumb. It's kind of embarrassing."

"How do you mean 'embarrassing,' Ronnie?" I asked.

He looked right at me, not at his classmates. "Well, okay," he said. "He's this black guy, and they make him sound like a fool. And he gets dogged. Know what I mean?"

Mary opened her book. "Like on page fifty-nine," she said. "When they argue about French? This is a place where it seems that Jim really doesn't look wise at all."

We spent the period on chapter 14, debating whether Twain had drawn, through Huck's voice, a fool, as Ronnie had said. This scene shows us two debates between Jim and Huck, one about whether French people speak a different language. After Meredith read the scene aloud, wincing as she said the last line of the chapter, we paused. "Who wins this argument?" I asked.

Amari offered, "I think Jim does. I mean, he's wrong, but he wins." His classmates agreed.

"But he's so ignorant. I mean, who doesn't know that people speak different languages?" Ronnie pressed.

"Well, if you'd been a slave . . . I mean, Jim's not worldly, but that's not the same as being stupid," Amari said.

"But aren't we thinking too much about this?" Rachel asked. "I mean, if you have to do this much work to see how he's not stupid, then isn't he probably just a racist caricature?"

I asked, "So why does Twain end the chapter with Huck saying, 'You can't learn a nigger to argue'?"

Ronnie sat up straight and then moved downward toward his desk with each word. "Because . . . he's . . . a racist!"

Dylan raised his hand. "Ronnie's right. Huck is racist. But he says that because he has lost the argument, and the only thing he has to fall back on is his whiteness. So, Huck is racist, but that's what Twain is trying to show us here." I could tell that not everyone agreed.

~

The more my kids and I read and talked, the more I was struck by the multiple ways in which Jim undermines the stereotype of the submissive minstrel he sometimes resembles. Not a passive subject at all, Jim has a voice: he uses it to argue outspokenly with Huck. Also, in his display of love for his own children, and not just for a white boy, Jim debunks the myth that the enslaved didn't have the same familial bonds as whites. In the ultimate act of defiance for an enslaved person, Jim escapes (he tells Huck that he "lit out," in fact), and, further, he promises that he will buy or steal his wife and children from their owners if necessary. He says early in the text, "I owns myself" (36), and he means it.

When he appears to be silent or caricatured, Jim is often wearing a mask of subservience, which is crucial to his survival while enslaved, and then to his escape. We hear Jim's words as told to us by Huck, but, as my students pointed out early in our reading, Huck does not always understand the subtext, so we as readers can see what Huck does not. We risk underestimating Jim if we hear only what Huck hears and ignore Jim's "double-voicing."

The class spent a lot of time with the most important moments of Huck and Jim's relationship. We talked about the scene in which Jim and Huck lose each other in the fog. When Huck returns to the raft to find Jim asleep, he plays a nasty trick on him, pretending that Jim has dreamed the whole terrifying scene. Jim is ecstatic to see Huck and launches into an interpretation of his dream. When Huck points out the debris in the boat, the physical proof of Jim's memory, Jim doesn't miss a beat:

> He looked at me steady, without ever smiling and says "What do dey stan' for? I's gwyne to tell you. When I got all wore out wid work, en wid de callin' for you, en went to sleep, my heart wuz mos' broke bekase you wuz los', . . . En when I wake up en fine you back agin', all safe en soun', de tears come en I could a got down on my knees and kiss' yo' foot I's so thankful. En all you

wuz thinkin' 'bout wuz how you could make a fool uv ole Jim wid a lie. Dat truck dah is *trash*; en trash is what people is dat puts dirt on de head er dey fren's en makes 'em ashamed." (65)

Here Jim not only stands up for himself but teaches Huck a lesson in humanity; he tries to undo Tom Sawyer's lessons that life and everything in it are a game. Jim asserts his authority, even invoking the insult "white trash." He declares that they are friends and demands better treatment from Huck.

Throughout the book, Huck learns and grows, but not enough to reject the moral code of the world in which he lives. Even when he decides "All right, I'll *go* to hell" (162), compromising his eternal soul to free Jim, it's important that he does not say, "All those people are wrong. Slavery is evil, I am doing good by counteracting it." Huck's sense of his own position, that he is low-down and ignorant, and was "brung up wicked" (160), does not allow him to privilege his own views vis-à-vis matters of morality. Huck cannot fully reject white superiority.

My students saw both sides of the question in the depiction of Jim. They asked, "If we have to be such good readers to understand Jim as subversive, is this book effective or responsible social criticism?"

The class and I longed for an African American character who did not wear the "clown suit," as Morrison calls it, however many holes it offers into Jim's real mind and character. We noted the free African American professor described with loathing by Huck's father; we noted Jack, who helps Huck and shows the community of the slaves. But still, we longed for a clear picture of Jim, or an unadulterated, incontrovertible view of the full humanity of an African American character.

～

My students could not have known the relief I felt in their presence, given the personal torture I was enduring in endless meetings. Class time became a refuge for me, as I relished even our most boring talks and our most difficult ones. In each and every meeting I continued to have with my colleagues, I tried to explain why I was teaching *Huck Finn* and how I understood the text. I argued that no one would advocate removing the subject of slavery from our history courses on the basis that it was a racist institution. So why should we avoid reading books that dealt with the same issues?

While the adults resisted and refused specific text-based conversations, my students and I continued to discuss the details of the book. We agreed; we disagreed; we struggled. We moved from the text to reading some of the literature surrounding it. We talked about how *Huck Finn* had been banned in many schools.

"But that's such a backwater thing to do," Dylan said. "That could never happen in a place like this."

∼

The kids had finished reading *Huck Finn*.

"I hate the end!" Elizabeth said to start our conversation. There was much murmured agreement.

Many of the kids were rightly appalled by the game Tom plays with Jim's fate, endlessly complicating his release to the point of endangering all of their lives and Jim's freedom. They complained, "Huck went along with it! Why?"

Huck's voice does indeed disappear in the last chapters of the book; he passes for Tom, while Tom is disguised as his own brother. All this leaves little room for Huck, who still suffers from Tom worship. Both Huck and the reader have to be shaken from any thought of admiring or romanticizing Tom Sawyer and his brand of boyhood. For a brief moment, Huck thinks he has found a kindred spirit in Tom, a white boy who could help free an enslaved man. In the end, Huck learns that Tom's conscience does not operate like his own: Jim has been free all along, manumitted by Miss Watson's will, while Tom has been recklessly playing with his life.

Tom may symbolize the worst of the white status quo, a composite of the evils of the North and the South. In *The Jim Dilemma*, Jocelyn Chadwick-Joshua describes Tom as metonymic of "the (un)reconstructed South." She explains that Tom "relies on and perverts every concept on which the South presumably structured its mythic persona: pride, rightness, filial loyalty, honesty, and salvation" (*The Jim Dilemma: Reading Race in* Huckleberry Finn, Jocelyn Chadwick-Joshua [Jackson: University Press of Mississippi, 1998], 120). Like the North, Tom is pretending to emancipate Jim, but only because it serves his pleasure. Historically, when it was politically expedient, the North abandoned Reconstruction. In the book Tom wistfully wishes that he and Huck could go on freeing Jim forever, even leaving him to future (white) generations to (pretend to) free. In Tom's disgusting fantasy, Jim would be left in a state of perpetual near freedom, toyed with for the amusement of whites. Especially after the end of Reconstruction in 1877, this state of pretend freedom in Tom's fantasy became a reality: the "freedmen" (and women, of course) were not free; they were reenslaved by sharecropping, the rise of the KKK, and then Jim Crow.

My students and I debated whether the end is happy. We asked where Huck would end up. We were pleased that he refuses to go along with Tom's version of things. We knew that Jim plans to free his wife and children by any means necessary, that he may be able to be reunited with his real family. We were glad that Huck does not give in to the society we know is wrong.

But the end rankled us as ambiguous. If we believe Huck, we expect that he will "light out for the Territory ahead of the rest," this time on land, but more profoundly alone than before. He can't stand civilization because he has learned what civilization entails: cruelty, abusive and hypocritical white fathers, bloody feuds among people who bring their guns to church and sacrifice the lives of their children, con artists, and a firm taboo against a continued real relationship with Jim. Alone, orphaned, still convinced of his own inadequacy but knowing he cannot go along with the ways of the world, Huck plans to "light out" in self-imposed exile.

∽

When we were finished with *Huck Finn* (the kids had written two essays, ten response journal entries, and a couple of freewrites; traced a theme; presented a group project; and read seven articles about the controversy surrounding the text) and poised to move on to the equally difficult territory of *Beloved,* I asked them to answer one last question about *Huck Finn:* whether I should include the book on my syllabus the next year, and whether reading it could damage any students.

My students advised that I teach *Huck Finn* again, with one notable exception. Many kids wrote about the value of the conversations we had had around the book, about the rewards of talking in detail about such a complex work. Most kids cited our unusually "deep" level of discourse. Amy wrote that our *Huck Finn* discussions had been "the most important [she] had ever had in school."

To my question of whether it could be damaging, kids mostly answered that it couldn't, or not if it were taught carefully and well. But underneath these assertions, I sensed a recognition of the pain and difficulties of the text. Amari wrote that he and his classmates were "already mad desensitized," and Elizabeth claimed that they were "old enough" to read *Huck Finn.* They seemed to acknowledge but then dismiss that *Huck Finn* is indeed painful.

A more extreme manifestation of this—and much more upsetting to me—were assertions from a few of the white boys in the class that anyone who could possibly be hurt by *Huck Finn* must be deficient in some way. The most extreme of these came from Brian, who said that he doubted that anyone had been damaged by reading *Huck Finn,* but "those who were would be so weak emotionally and so undeveloped that they could be hurt by anything. To take the book away from most students because a few couldn't deal with the struggles of real life is unjust and wrong." By "most" I think he meant "white." Were some of my students still clinging to their assertion that racism didn't exist anymore and that African Americans in particular should "get over it"?

Then came the only clear statement of distress, from Monique. She said that reading *Huck Finn* made her feel "hurt and insulted," that Twain used Huck's voice to "deem black people as being stupid and very ill mannered. (Monique is far from "weak" in Brian's terms). Monique further wrote that if she were the teacher, she would not allow the book on her syllabus, citing it as misleading: "Imagine having a student who has never had real contact with a black person. They would have a huge misconception of how blacks really act. It makes blacks look like they're tagalongs and don't have a mind of their own."

When I talked to Monique about the views she expressed, she said that she meant them in general terms, and that at our school it was acceptable to teach the book because no one there was racially isolated. I was unconvinced, struck by the vehemence of her writing.

∽

In my multiple meetings with adults, I was frequently conscious of some undercurrent, some unsaid something that lurked beneath what people were saying. We talked at crosscurrents. What I did hear loud and clear, from an African American administrator specifically, was a resounding mantra: "This stuff hurts." And one time, "Slavery still hurts." "Of course," I said. "That's why I'm talking about it." And occasionally I felt we were saying exactly the same thing, and the struggle was about who should get to say it, when, and to whom.

I remembered my mentor's warning, which I had heard but not heeded. Still, I felt the level of engagement my students had achieved outweighed these less than comfortable interactions with adults. But the struggle was taking its toll on me personally.

∽

I quit. More specifically, I took a leave of absence and moved to Cape Cod for an overdue adventure of my own. I had long planned to do this, but the events of that year gave me the resolve to leave the school. I finished the school year, said good-bye to my kids, and lit out.

Ronnie, Jeff, and Miguel, were the only students in the class not to pass. They did not take the AP exam because they went with the diversity consultant on a field trip for the two weeks before the test. After about the third quarter, they stopped reading, stopped doing homework, and came to class late. The other students of color, African American, biracial, Cape Verdean, Haitian American, and African, all passed the class and took the AP exam. Monique, Hannah, Amari, Katrina, and the others remained part of the group. But the three students, the very three who had come to talk with me so openly earlier in the year, disappeared from view. They were still friendly with me, but a distance had grown between us, and the time I would have needed to devote to them outside the classroom was taken up in endless meetings. The adults who could have been helping me address the real problems inherent in such classroom discussions did not.

It was late June when Jeff and Miguel came to talk to me again, with Jeff's school-successful girlfriend in tow. I was taking down my posters, stripping the walls of student work.

"Emileeee," Miguel said in a low voice as he came in, Jeff dropping Keisha's hand as they walked through the door.

We sat to talk.

"Why are you leaving the school?" Jeff asked me, looking down at my desk, where students had scrawled my name and theirs in cheery neon letters on the plastic shelf lining I had affixed.

I looked at him closely while he looked down. "For a lot of reasons. I need some time off. I need to plan to go to graduate school. There's a lot going on here at the school."

Jeff looked at me. "I'm asking because people are saying that you're leaving because . . . I was just worried that you were leaving because of something I did, and I didn't mean to hurt you or make you leave."

As I looked at him evenly, I crumbled inside. We had failed him so miserably. What I had warned of had come to pass: the kids had been used as pawns in a dispute between adults that was ostensibly about their best interests. And they knew it.

He went on. "I just think maybe some of what I said was misrepresented. I didn't say you were racist or bad or anything. All I ever said was that I felt uncomfortable, and that was true. I did feel that way, and that's all I ever said."

"You should be able to say that," I managed. "You should be able to say you are uncomfortable without being afraid of anything. It's our job to create a space for you to be able to say that, and to work on it."

Jeff talked about why he had felt uncomfortable; he presented a litany of, in his estimation, hard-to-take texts about race; the burden of being one of only two black boys in the class; the amount of work;

the intellectual or emotional somersaults it took to understand what we were reading. I thanked him for coming to talk to me, thanked Keisha and Miguel for accompanying him.

When they left, I locked my classroom door, something I never do. I sat at my desk, out of view of the panel of window in the door, with my head in my hands. I must have sat for twenty minutes. I felt sad for Jeff that he had gone around feeling responsible for my leaving, impressed that he had come to talk to me anyway, and angry and disappointed in our adult inability to take better care of our kids; I was also struck by how teaching a book could have caused all this turmoil.

~

Here, in self-imposed exile, I feel like Huck. I dropped all my responsibilities at the school, cut off my ties with the civilization I had known, and retreated to my own Territory. Now I have to decide what to do next.

Toni Morrison writes that "silence and evasion" pervade discussions about race, that "ignoring race is understood to be a graceful, even generous, liberal gesture." But this habit "forecloses adult discourse." No one bothers those white teachers who "gracefully" ignore race altogether. No one challenges the teacher at our school who has always taught *Huck Finn,* offering her kids the abridged, denuded version of the text, teaching it as if it is all about a boy's journey to freedom, never talking about race. I could leave that to teachers of color and retreat to so-called white matters, as if our histories were extricable, distinct. As if the magic of Shakespeare, the music of *The Odyssey,* and the wit of Mark Twain belonged to whites alone.

In the sequel to *The Adventures of Huckleberry Finn,* called *Tom Sawyer Abroad,* Twain retreats from the possibility of freedom for Jim and Huck. Jim does not fight to free his family; instead, he accompanies the boys on an adventure, this time in a hot-air balloon. Huck does not break free of civilization; he returns to it without mentioning his former plan to "light out." We are bound to society: we must live in it or die.

So instead of dropping out altogether, we must find a way to stay and fight ignorance and racism. In the fall, I will return to teaching, but not on Tom Sawyer's terms. I will take the lessons I have learned from my students and continue teaching *Huck Finn,* now well aware of the kinds of trouble that can beset the fragile raft of open classroom conversation.

• TALKING BACK: MAKING MORAL CHOICES IN AN IMMORAL WORLD •

• JOURNEY TO ADULTHOOD •

• SEE ALSO BANNED BOOKS •

SUFFERING UNTO TRUTH: DO YOU THINK YOUR FUTURE IS FATED?

Aeschylus's *Oresteia*

Rick Ayers

Dear gods, set me free from all the pain," declares the watchman at the beginning of *Aga-memnon*, setting the stage for a most dreadful story, one that confronts us brutally with the horrors of death and a life filled with wrong choices.

I began to wonder if this was the right way to start my eleventh-grade World Literature class. Yes, the trilogy *The Oresteia* is a classic and would set a great benchmark for the year. And the local theater, the Berkeley Repertory Theatre, was planning to present the whole trilogy in the spring.

But this was going to be a hard ride. The junior class of Communication Arts and Sciences (CAS) was coming to me with a bad reputation. They were the "problem" class, the ones who drove their freshman teacher crazy, who inspired other teachers to try to get out of teaching them. In our diverse high school, it was also the class with the highest number of working-class kids and "at risk" kids and the lowest level of literacy and academic preparation. The majority of the kids were African American, which made this class more like the "urban" side of Berkeley as opposed to the "suburban" population.

Could we really jump off with a story of about a warrior king returning from Troy and being slaughtered by his wife and her lover, with the subsequent revenge killing by the cursed couple's son with the aid of his sister? I have always been an advocate of more texts by authors of color, always coming down against the "dead white men" curriculum in the canonical debates. Still, it turned out that many of the classics were not a "bitter medicine" that had to be swallowed; for one thing, they're filled with appealing topics like sex and violence. People who talk about the corrupting influence of rap lyrics and violent movies ought to take a gander at the Greeks. And the classics were not exercises in bowing to authority. The Greeks were above all doubtful, suspicious, and critical of authority. I did not believe this class needed to be confined to tales of ghetto heroism and tragedy. We could travel back 2,500 years and 4,500 miles to some of the foundational works of "Western civilization" and find relevant and powerful tales.

Robert Fagles, in the introduction to his 1976 translation, declares that "*The Oresteia* is our rite of passage from savagery to civilization." Yes, in fact it is the story of the first democratic court system. In this trilogy, a seemingly endless cycle of violence is plaguing the House of Atreus, with one revenge killing following after another. Finally wise Athena, patron goddess of Athens, comes down and declares it is time for brute force to step aside. Both sides of the blood feud will argue their cases. But here's the real twist. It is neither she nor Zeus who will decide. A jury from the audience will be impaneled (an early case of audience participation) and judge the case. Suddenly in *The Eumenides*, the third installment of the trilogy, the play changes from a gore fest to a courtroom drama. What a revelation. We don't have to slaughter each other. There is a way out.

This was the secular urge of the Greeks in its full glory. They would rely neither on the gods nor on brute force to settle things. No, reason and persuasion would decide the case. And we would be freed of the need for more killing, more revenge, and more horror. This was a way in, and I saw the way we would work in relevance to the students' lived lives. I read the play, making marks and noting themes. But I still did not grasp the play in all its resonance. That would wait until the class began reading it aloud together.

• THE CYCLE OF REVENGE •

By the second day of class, we had begun reading *Agamemnon*. I'm always anxious to start reading aloud together and encounter whatever difficulties and confusions come up.

So, we plunged in, beginning to work our way along, the Fagles translation just noble enough but also accessible. The animal imagery jumped out at the students. The chorus describes the two commanders of the Greek forces, the brothers Agamemnon and Menelaus, as twin eagles, fierce and merciless. In fact, the chorus describes the vision of a seer, who spied two eagles swooping down and tearing open a pregnant hare, scattering her unborn babes on the ground in a bloody mess. "Eeew," exclaimed Angela, throwing back her tie-dyed scarf, "how gross." Gross, yes indeed, but all I could think of with a certain amount of glee was, *It's going to get much worse.*

They had yet to encounter the flashback, the story of how Atreus, the twin kings' father, brought a curse on his house by engaging in a quarrel with his brother Thyestes and one day serving him a dinner in which he had cooked up Thyestes' own children in a stew. They were captivated by the tale—this was no longer obscure Greek literature but an over-the-top horror story.

Now that they were involved with the play, the problem statement, the overriding issue, made its appearance. It seemed that all the horror was tied to an endless cycle of revenge. And teenagers know this paradigm only too well. How many times have the adults broken up futile fights and confrontations, only to have the participants complain, "Well, he did this to me first," or "But she did that to my sister." Somehow payback was reason enough to do something stupid. Maybe Aeschylus could help us think about this pattern and how to break it.

After all, the doomed people in the House of Atreus had plenty to be angry about, far more than a playground slight.

The main action of *Agamemnon* (the first play of the Oresteia trilogy) is that the queen, Clytemnestra, kills her husband on his arrival back, victorious, from the Trojan War. Agamemnon was a leader of the Greek coalition fighting against the Trojans and has fought for ten long years, only to be cut down the day he arrives home. Why the murder? Well, Clytemnestra was upset, to say the least, that her husband had sacrificed their beautiful teenage daughter, Iphigenia, to secure a safe ocean passage on the eve of the war. Then again, she also has a motive for killing Agamemnon's new concubine, Cassandra, and installing her own new paramour as the king. In the next play, *The Libation Bearers*, Agamemnon's daughter and son, Electra and Orestes, avenge their father's murder by killing Clytemnestra. In *The Eumenides*, Clytemnestra's ghost and the avenging earth goddesses (the Furies) come after Orestes to kill him in vengeance for the matricide. Here wise Athena intervenes and sets up a tribunal, to stop the cycle of violence and determine a final and just resolution.

~

As we were reading the first pages, I gave the students the assignment to write a personal reflection. They were to tell a story, a narrative, about an example of a cycle of revenge—how people behave in loyalty to their own group by getting back at, getting revenge on, the "outsider," or "other," group.

One of my students, Francisco, was always quiet and seldom responded to writing assignments. He came to class regularly but stayed out of discussions—sitting in the back with his Dickies work pants, clean-pressed white T-shirt, and short hair slicked straight back. This time he handed in something right away, and he was clearly in touch with the danger in the theme. He wrote,

> The cycle of revenge is an extremely dangerous thing to be part of, and it has a lot of consequences for you and even your family. The Norteños and Sureños live the cycle of violence and

revenge every day. The cycle never ends. It keeps going back and forth. Both sides are living the life of [*The*] *Oresteia*.

The Norteños and Sureños can be extremely powerful when it comes to violence and revenge. There is this saying by the Norteños, "You take out one of ours, we take out ten of yours."

"And I say rush in now, catch them red-handed, butchery running on their blades." I chose this quote [from *Agamemnon*] because many Sureños and Norteños get caught red-handed in their rivals' turf. Some get caught red-handed by going to and tagging on their rivals' turf. They can also get caught (slippin') just being on your rivals' turf. This has happened to a lot of my friends. I heard stories of them getting jumped, stabbed, and shot by rivals. They also went back for payback, but they never think of the consequences. While getting paid back, sometimes the rivals come back and sometimes they don't. But they come back some day, the cycle just never ends.

The stuff we were dealing with was real. Francisco dug right into the sense of futility and frustration engendered by the cycle of violence in his life and found pieces of Aeschylus's writing that speak directly to him. I only hoped that he could stay with it through all three plays, with the resolution, the breaking of the cycle, and the achievement of peace and a just society. Was it possible that he would be able to apply the Greek solution in West Berkeley?

Aysha, the slam poet and African American radical of the class, took Francisco's point, written in the privacy of his paper, and brought it into the discussion in the classroom. How do we understand revenge, even with kids on the playground? Is this something called human nature, or are we taught to do it? And isn't revenge sometimes justified—either to teach the wrongdoer or to gain some satisfaction? But who is the wronged one? There always seem to be eight sides to every story.

Big thoughts, and, yes, Francisco, Aysha, and Angela were right into them. The class was engaged, and I was holding my breath, hoping we could continue to surf this wave of interest.

Something about reading together, aloud, made all these new and fascinating connections jump out. Whereas academics read with a cool eye, high school students are fiercely present, always looking for the powerful connection to their lives. Aeschylus made them question their choices and their pride, made them wonder about impulsive actions and moderation, and made them consider the wisdom of their elders less dismissively.

We talked about theater, then and now. The earliest Greek theater festivals took place at the feast of Dionysus, the annual celebration of the harvest and wine, licentiousness, debauchery, wildness, and the unbridled id. The students were fascinated to hear about the tragedy competitions. Who says poetry is sullied by competition for money in slams? Such competition was good enough to create Aeschylus and Sophocles—not bad company. And of course each set of three tragedies was coupled with a comedy and a Satyr play. The latter, a wild physical comedy filled with sexual parading (how about those six-foot-long phalluses for a theater?), are always fascinating to high school students. We never, of course, stage such plays as part of our appreciation of Greek culture.

We were drawn into a long discussion about gender, especially as we read *Agamemnon*, the story of the murderous wife. The chorus tells a flashback tale in which the goddess Artemis requires the sacrifice of Iphigenia, Agamemnon and Clytemnestra's beautiful thirteen-year-old daughter, for the storms to abate and for the Greek ships to have smooth sailing to Troy. Aeschylus does not spare us the disgusting details. It's all there, the girl screaming, a gag stuffed in her mouth, her clothes torn off, her arms and legs bound, then the carving, and the blood. And with his commitment to the requirements of war—a task of state, "men's work"—Agamemnon has violated the laws of home, hearth, the center of life, and "women's rights."

The chorus, recounting the house gossip, laments, "A father's hands are stained, blood of a young girl streaks the altar. Pain both ways and what is worse? Desert the fleets, fail the alliance? No, but stop the winds with a virgin's blood? Feed their lust, their fury? Feed their fury! Law is law! Let all go well!" (l. 210).

So as we were reading, a new theme emerged, the men versus the women, the question of patriarchy. According to one reading, *The Oresteia* explains that women's power (represented by Clytemnestra as well as her earth goddesses, the Furies) must be overthrown—even if it is painful—for civilization to be established. In this play we see the struggle between the old, communal, and tribal society and the new imperial civilization of the polis. Just as the old earth goddesses, Gaia and the Furies, were overthrown by the Olympians Zeus and Apollo, so the mother-right must be overthrown for the men to carry out their imperial tasks. Looking at the depredations of the modern empires, from Britain to Germany and the United States itself, many students wonder whether tribal, prehistorical societies may have been better— for human life and for nature.

But that neat story doesn't quite do justice to the unruly forces at work here. Clytemnestra's adultery, her maternal attachment to Iphigenia, and her murderous fury point to different directions, at least to modern ears.

There is something frightening in the women of *The Oresteia*— Clytemnestra with her terrible power, Electra with her strong will, and Cassandra with her horrific visions. It is as if the men are afraid of the very passion, the very sexuality, of the women, and these must be controlled and repressed.

Angela and Aysha pick up on this. Why did Aeschylus make Clytemnestra out to be such a bitch? Aeschylus even leveled the accusation that a strong woman, one who resists the sacrifice of her daughter, is not feminine enough. After Clytemnestra's first speech, the chorus leader remarks, "spoken like a man, my lady." Maybe she's not so bad, the students argued; maybe she has a grievance that no one will listen to. How would the play look if a woman had written it?

And most strikingly to me, we grappled with death.

When Agamemnon returns victorious, Clytemnestra urges him to enter the palace by walking on the red tapestry, a long, embroidered royal rug she has prepared for him. In words rife with double meaning (foreshadowing the blood of Agamemnon that is about to flow), she says, as she rolls out the tapestry, "Let the red stream flow and bear him home to the home he never hoped to see—Justice lead him in" (l. 904). Agamemnon is anxious, not sure he should step on such a beautiful tapestry, afraid such an act would be too proud, too risky. He says, "What am I, some barbarian peacocking out of Asia? Never cross my paths with robes and draw the lightning [never deck me out like a god and attract the wrath, and lightning, of Zeus]. Never, only the gods deserve the pomps of honor" (l. 915). The comment on the "barbarian peacocking" refers to Mongol and Persian warriors who dressed in all their finery, with full makeup, when going to war.

Here, Clytemnestra has her way. With a combination of bullying and flattery, she persuades Agamemnon to go against his better judgment and act like a god. Ah, then his downfall is sealed. He steps out of his chariot onto the red tapestry, walks into his house, and is slaughtered in the bathtub by his wife.

At this point, the dramatic irony, as well as personal recognition, became real for the class. Anthony remarked, "Yes, you can always try to avoid this error or that error. But we are human. We never know the future or what effect will be created by this or that action. So we are doomed to making the tragic error. Only the powerful ones, the arrogant ones, make the error in a big, loud, public way."

The class seemed to resist the play. "Why is there so much death, so much slaughter in these things?" intoned Aysha. "Why is Western literature always about killing, suicide, and despair?"

"I'm not sure," I backpedaled. "Maybe it's because it would be boring to have a simple happy story, two people falling in love, walking off into the sunset, and living happily ever after. Where's the fun in that?" But there was more.

Jesse challenged me: "These guys are obsessed with death. Why?"

I wondered too. Maybe they knew death more intimately. Maybe we should too. Perhaps our sanitized lives, I suggested, where the infirm are sent away to die in isolation, allow us to live in denial. People gather in the theater and weep over the most extreme situations as a way of facing the terror of inevitable death together.

From a modern sensibility, the terror at our mortality, at our being lost to the world, is an existential crisis. It is the story of death, of how we face it or turn away from it. The Greek tragedies make us take a good long look at our mortality. Maybe on other days, engrossed in workaday trivialities, we don't think about death. But when we are most in touch with it, most aware, we look into the yawning abyss, and we quake. The class agreed to read on, this time with a bit less bravado.

Clytemnestra crows about her power and her husband's household, declaring her pride and hubris without hesitation. "Our lives are based on wealth, my king, the gods have seen to that ... and you are Zeus when Zeus tramples the bitter virgin grapes"(ll. 960ff.). But the chorus is still frightened, still worried. "Stark terror whirls the brain and the end is coming, Justice comes to birth" (l. 998). The old men fear the specific horror about to happen but also bemoan the fate of all mortals, what Unamuno called the tragic sense of life, the fact that we must die: "But a man's life-blood is dark and mortal. Once it wets the earth, what song can sing it back?" (l. 1018).

Then Clytemnestra tries to entice Cassandra (Agamemnon's mistress and war captive, the daughter of Troy's Priam) to follow Agamemnon into the house. Cassandra is silent, and Clytemnestra quickly tires of trying to engage her and leaves. The chorus leader then speaks to Cassandra, trying to show pity and concern. Cassandra, however, was given the power of prophecy by Apollo and dreads going inside. Her first words are a half-mad scream, "Aieeeee! Earth—Mother—Curse of the Earth—Apollo, Apollo!" (l. 1071). She speaks with the leader, always emitting sharp cries and visions of the future as well as the past of the House of Atreus. This dramatic scene has Cassandra pitching herself around onstage, seeing the horrors of the future. "She is the snare," she cries, referring to Clytemnestra, "the bedmate, death mate, murder's strong right arm!" (l. 1117).

The chorus is confused by all of this and doubts the veracity of her words. Cassandra raises another concern of the Greeks that is familiar in our postmodern consciousness: what is true, what can we really know? The gods name things, and their words are true, but what words are we mortals to believe? "What good are the oracles to men? Words, more words, and the hurt comes on us, endless words and a seer's techniques have brought us terror and the truth" (l. 1135). Cassandra's vision becomes even more opaque, more surreal. She screams, "Flare up once more, my oracle!" and then she conjures a vision from hell, of dancing Furies, legions of men killed in battle, blood for blood. She then describes, in horrendous detail, the feast at which Atreus (Agamemnon's father) served his unsuspecting brother Aegisthus his own children in a stew.

Cassandra predicts her own death but also knows that Orestes will return and kill Clytemnestra and her lover. "There will come another to avenge us, born to kill his mother, born his father's champion" (l. 1302). The leader asks the same question the students asked: "If you see it coming, clearly, how can you go to your own death, like a beast to the altar driven on by god, and hold your head so high?" (l. 1320). Cassandra explains that her time has come, and it is best to go out with honor. She enters the house, where she smells death. She ends her time onstage with an evocation of the existential dilemma: "Oh men, your destiny. When all is well the shadow can overturn it. When trouble comes, a stroke of the wet sponge, and the picture's blotted out. And that, I think, that breaks the heart" (l. 1350).

～

I asked students to do a freewrite on what they felt they had learned about Greek culture and values. Angela wrote:

> Greek culture. Intense. If I lived there then, well, I guess I wouldn't live for very long unless I set up a mafia or something. Jewish mafia in Greece.
>
> Greeks, if they saw so much death, why didn't they just stop? Clytemnestra killed because her daughter was murdered, but then to save her own neck she would have killed another one of her children (Orestes). Make any sense? No. Neither do the Greeks.
>
> A culture based on love and hate, revenge, ruled by Zeus, whose servants are women. The men rule over everything, like dogs gone wild, killing whatever gets in their way. People

have others as property, and the more property you have the better the people fight over property and power. And love and hate and lust. Life is a death sentence if you are in the family of Agamemnon.

It's a tradition, a traditional curse that falls upon houses struggling with one another for the power to be in control.

Death reaches people so extremely that that is all they can see. Death for death, life for life.

Well, gosh, I thought, *maybe I have been having a different experience with these plays than the students.* The Greek tragedies are painful, ghastly really. And many students commented that the Greeks seem to be reveling in death and destruction. *Have I been teaching this stuff wrong? What about the soaring insights of the Greek concept of love? What about the noble ideas of humanism and science? Does it look to the class like a deadly world of mafia terror?*

But when I looked further at Angela's wonderful reflection, written in a few minutes, I wondered. The tragedian has succeeded in weaving a picture of desperation, of despair, of the terrible downfall that mortals suffer. It is a world in which "men rule over everything, like dogs," and they fight over property and power. Well, this wasn't so unfamiliar. The dog reference fitted, too, because some of these plays demonstrate the dangers of an unchecked id, the violence and selfishness of desire.

I am older and, at least by degree, closer to death. So I contemplate these things, the existential black hole we peer into, wondering if it does end in dust. Teenagers are famous for living in an eternal present, seemingly immortal. But in reality they think about death all the time; they are just reaching the age where they can wonder deeply about it. Sometimes, perhaps, they want to look death in the eye and challenge it. Even though we adults shake our fingers at them and remind them of the dangers of fast cars, AIDS, violence, and cigarettes, sometimes they take these risks precisely to face down death, to dance with it, to challenge it, and sometimes to embrace it.

So Aeschylus has ground Angela's face in some pretty terrible thoughts. Great literature takes these thoughts out of the secret re-cesses of the mind and makes us take a good, hard look at them.

But on second thought, I could see that the Greeks had taken An-gela somewhere else. They had made her cry out (as Athena does), "When does it all stop, the killing, the tragedy, the cycle of revenge? Who is the one with the strength to stop it?" Yes, that's the question. And she couldn't have done a better job of setting up *The Eumenides*, the denouement of the trilogy, the resolution of the cycle of revenge. For Athena calls a tribunal composed of a jury of mortal citizens to review the various crimes (complete with a prosecutor and a defense attorney, like an Olympian version of the TV show *The Practice*). And we put an end to the violence. We establish order and civilization and human rights.

No, we do not escape the horrors of death. Part of the story is the encounter with mortality and a search for order and peace and love.

• SEEING *THE ORESTEIA* ONSTAGE •

By the end of October, we had finished with the plays and had moved on to other works, other texts, other discussions. But the story of Aga-memnon, Clytemnestra, and the whole cursed House of Atreus re-mained as a reference point for the rest of the year. When we were studying Latin America, we dived into the magical realism of Pablo Neruda's poetry as well as the small Mexican novel *Esperanza's Box of Saints*, by María Amparo Escandón. This was far from the Greeks, to be sure, but again we encountered cycles of revenge, the women's cri-tique of patriarchal power, and the grand mystery of death.

∼

The Berkeley Repertory Theatre presented Aeschylus's masterpiece a few months later. When *Agamemnon* finally opened, we were thrilled to be in the first student audience to attend the play. The play was per-formed at the new stage that the Rep had built, which they were in-augurating with the oldest surviving play. They performed the first tragedy on its own, and a week later they presented the other two, *The Libation Bearers* and *The Eumenides*.

When the day of the performance finally came, the whole class was excited. For students at a big school like Berkeley High, just getting off the campus is a treat. Yes, it was going to be a big old Greek tragedy, but they were ready, they knew what to expect. Except that they didn't, since the actors and directors impart so much to the performance.

We had gone over some of the main discussions, reread a few final papers, and discussed what to expect before heading to the theater.

The students filed into the new theater, a large venue with soaring seats that made everyone feel close to the front. There were the CAS juniors, the CAS freshmen, and the advanced Latin students. Their teacher, Ms. Alexander, always made sure she took them to classic plays, Greek or Latin, to broaden their experience with ancient culture.

The whole front of the stage was covered by a massive stone wall, representing the city of Argos. The students bent together and whispered, "Look, there's the watchman. Remember the beginning?"

As the play progressed, I became delighted with the production. I also kept looking back at the students to see what they were taking in. It was all there: "We must suffer, suffer unto truth"; "By the sword you did your work and by the sword you die"; "Our lives are pain, what part not come from god?"; "Words, endless words I've said to serve the moment—now it makes me proud to tell the truth"; "Call no man blest until he ends his live in peace, fulfilled."

The only thing the students could not abide was the depiction of Cassandra. She was the seer, a visionary who was cursed with the fact that no one would believe her. She was also a bit mad, a wild and crazy spectacle. And I had been told she would be completely naked onstage. When she emerged, the students were shocked and angry, but not by the nudity, which became secondary. No, what bothered them was how horrid, filthy, disheveled, and "torn up" Cassandra looked. They were expecting to see a brilliant seer, a beautiful concubine of

Agamemnon, the sister of Helen. Instead, Cassandra looked like a refugee from the schizophrenic ward in the movie *One Flew over the Cuckoo's Nest*. The students looked scandalized.

Of course, the nudity was the director's choice. Cassandra staggered, bellowed, and screamed. The students, in turn, squirmed and mumbled ("Oh, no, that ain't right," one of them said). Well, they were learning; that is part of the theatergoing experience. You interact with what's onstage. You like one thing but don't like something else. Personally, I loved it and fought back tears through the whole ending —tears at the horror and beauty of it and at being there with a group of sixteen- and seventeen-year-olds taking in the whole spectacle.

When the final curtain came down, we heard thundering applause. Students clapped, stood up, laughed. Many had never been at a performance like this and were delighted to see the actors come back onstage, in their own identities now, smiling at the audience, applauding back, and taking bows in pairs, individually, and as an ensemble. *A good curtain call always makes a good play greater,* I thought.

As we were leaving, I asked Ms. Alexander's Latin students, some of whom I knew, "How did you like it?" "Hated it!" responded Chloe. "Hella boring, God!" Others chimed in, "What was that?" "I thought it would never end!" *Well,* I thought, *apparently they weren't engaged.* After all, they had gone over the plot of the play only the day before. But when you think about it, not much happens. A guy comes home after lots of choral chanting and discussions by this and that person, and when he goes inside he is murdered by his wife; his lover is murdered too. End of play. But there is so much there, so much going on. I felt bad for the Latin students because they are, after all, mostly 4.0 students. But they did not have time to delve into the play, to really understand it. The freshmen in CAS were getting more out of it.

That would have been the end of it except for an unfortunate encounter I had with a chaperone, a parent of one of the Latin students, a few days later. She stopped me in the hall and said, "Listen, Rick, I just have to tell you I was upset with your students. You know, they were chatting, moaning, wiggling throughout the play. It does not reflect well on our school if our students don't know how to be an audience." I was dumbfounded. Sad. Embarrassed. I mumbled an apology and hurried on.

Later, though, I felt angry. There were the poor Latin students, rushed along on an AP schedule, memorizing facts but never having time to reflect, to dig in. They hated the play but knew how to feign interest. In fact, one of the skills of an advanced student is to pretend to be interested. What a loss for them.

And there were my kids, engaged with the play and with each other and a bit more wiggly. I'm sure some of them were out of it, and at least one fell asleep. But what the hell, we had spent months on this, we had met some of the actors, and the kids were digging it. They did not just love it; they were connecting their experience to Aeschylus, thinking about how to live as a result of this experience. Here were many more African American and Latino students, students who have a tradition of the black church, of call and response, of interacting with the stage. Yes, sometimes there were audible responses to the action onstage—as opposed to the polite hands in the lap. What the parent objected to was not that my students were disengaged but the manner in which they were engaged. I would venture to guess that the Greek audience of three thousand years ago was more like my students, loud, restless, likely to respond audibly to something they liked or didn't like. My kids, however, were getting stereotyped. They were the "bad" ones at the play.

But the real experience of those CAS juniors and *The Oresteia* was not that we could bring the classics to a group of diverse students. It was that a diversity of students could come to *The Oresteia* and bring everything—their concerns, their anger, their brilliance—and make it real and important, the way theater is supposed to be. The classics are not ossified, but our notion of how to teach them often is.

My experience with this group of students and *The Oresteia* convinced me that great literature is timeless not because it is inaccessible but precisely because each audience, each generation, makes compelling meaning of the piece. And I'm certain that any student, from any background, can derive rich and important experiences from such works if he or she can get with the right group—a classroom, a family, or friends—to voyage out and discover the power of literature.

• HUBRIS AND NEMESIS •

Aeschylus,	*The Oresteia*, 61
Dostoyevsky, Fyodor,	*Crime and Punishment*, 133
Heaney, Seamus,	*The Cure at Troy*, 143
Melville, Herman,	*Moby Dick*, 158
Tartt, Donna,	*The Secret History*, 173

• IS YOUR FUTURE FATED? •

Aeschylus,	*The Oresteia*, 61
Armstrong, Karen,	*The Battle for God*, 122
Camus, Albert,	*The Stranger*, 128
Chopin, Kate,	*The Awakening*, 130
Coelho, Paulo,	*The Alchemist*, 130
Dry, Richard,	*Leaving*, 133
Fitzgerald, F. Scott,	*The Great Gatsby*, 136
Maclean, Norman,	*Young Men and Fire*, 155
Quinn, Daniel,	*Ishmael*, 165
Russo, Richard,	*Empire Falls*, 167
Wharton, Edith,	*The House of Mirth*, 178
Williams, John A.,	*The Man Who Cried I Am*, 178

• THE CYCLE OF VIOLENCE •

Aeschylus,	*The Oresteia*, 61
Burgess, Anthony,	*A Clockwork Orange*, 127
Crane, Stephen,	*The Red Badge of Courage*, 131
Dry, Richard,	*Leaving*, 133

SPIRITUAL JOURNEYS: WHAT IS THE PATH TO ENLIGHTENMENT?

Rudolfo Anaya's *Bless Me, Ultima*

Bonnie Katzive

I TEACH STUDENTS WHO are, on the whole, pretty much the same as I was in ninth grade: Anglo, suburban, and middle and upper-middle class. Our ninth-grade curriculum is fairly typical: short stories, a few plays, a poetry unit, a few novels. The standards are *Romeo and Juliet, Of Mice and Men,* and *The Miracle Worker.* There is a lot of drama and emotion in these works, of course, but the core issues are fairly obvious and bold. These books have subtlety in their language and characterization, but not so much in their ideas. It is all great stuff, but most of the texts don't really shake up my students' outlook. And, in our district, students' outlooks on literature and the world get shaken up, big time, when they hit tenth grade and take a World Literature course that starts with *The Epic of Gilgamesh* and ends with modernist novels, with challenging stops at Confucius, Dante, Jonathan Swift, and Franz Kafka.

For my ninth-grade students, *Bless Me, Ultima,* with its complex issues and challenging narrative style, opens a door into the unfamiliar. As Andrew said in class one day, "This book is strange; it isn't like anything I've ever read before. I'm not sure I understand it, but I want to." And so, we dive into the water.

The story, a seminal work of Chicano literature, takes place in a rural New Mexico town where Antonio Marez, age seven, lives with his father, a *vaquero* (rancher), and his mother, the daughter of farmers. The protagonist is confronted by forces beyond his control and must struggle to understand their ultimate meaning and power in his life. Anaya's novel is semi-autobiographical, blending characters and events based on his own childhood with the *cuentos* (folk tales) and mythical lore that he absorbed from his community. Like Anaya, Antonio feels conflicting pulls between tradition and modernity, between Spanish Catholic beliefs and Mexican Indian ones, and between the stable farmers' world and that of the restless *vaqueros*. Antonio's neighbors and brothers return from World War II as changed men unable to face their old world. And Antonio finds himself surrounded by people who expect him to become a priest and even ask him to hear their confessions. Antonio's dreams are intense, richly symbolic, and prophetic. In his dreams and in his waking life, he witnesses evil, murder, beauty, magic, and the mysteries of both his mother's Catholic faith and the pagan and magical traditions of the land.

Most of my students would not choose this book—a novel about a seven-year-old's crisis of faith—on their own. In fact, as we read the first few pages out loud in class, I could feel their interest starting to seep away. A few heads drooped on the desks. What if they didn't love this book that I found so enchanting? What if they didn't even like it? Perhaps they were thinking, *Another realistic novel set in a small working-class town? Didn't we read something like this in seventh grade? What does this have to do with me?*

And then we arrived at Antonio's first dream on page 4, and I stopped worrying. The dream is weird and includes strange, even taboo subjects like men firing rifles into the air to celebrate a birth and an argument over what to do with the placenta. Antonio's mother's family, the Lunas, want to take the afterbirth to their farm and bury it there, as a way to tie the infant Antonio to their land and their ways. His father's people, the Marez, declare him a *vaquero*, a wanderer, a descendant of conquistadores, and want to burn the placenta and scatter the ashes over the *llano* (New Mexican grasslands). The magical *curandera*, Ultima, who will figure large in the book, settles the debate in the dream by taking custody of the disputed and symbolic blood, declaring, "Only I will know his destiny."

Now the kids were hooked. The dream firmly declared to my class that this book would be different from books they had read before; Antonio has a destiny, and the road to it is fraught with danger.

Ultima herself is a mystery, yet a familiar comfort; grandmotherly yet fierce; gentle, yet in possession of immense power. She is a *curandera*, one of the healers of the Hispanic Southwest who blend traditional wisdom, herbal lore, magic, and even Catholicism in their medical practice. Even though the reader gets to know her, she remains enigmatic through much of the book. Will she survive accusations of witchcraft? Is she good or evil? Do good and evil exist?

Although standing around the baby arguing about what to do with the afterbirth is an uncommon theme of contemporary American experiences, the family conflict Antonio faces is familiar to that of many of my students: what do you do when your parents present radically different models of how to live?

We stopped reading for a while to share our experiences and ideas about parents. The conversation ranged from the trivial to the serious. Sarah told us how hard it is for her family to go to restaurants. Her working-class dad thinks McDonald's is fine and isn't quite sure what to do in a fancy restaurant; her refined mom, however, won't set foot in McDonald's and always wants to eat fine food. Katrina saved her restaurant stories for the more private venue of a writing assignment—she had spent innumerable hours sitting in a bar watching her dad get drunk—but it was a much more personal story than any she had cared to share with me before.

As we read on and Antonio continued to be racked by confusion over his path, my students wrote about their own role models in a brief personal essay. Their writing was full of declarations of love and admiration for parents, siblings, and friends but also revealed many of the challenges and complications in their lives. Jon, a bright, sensitive student who hates to work, admired his high-achieving older brother but feared the expectations that his brother's focus and ambition had created for him. Robert related to the way that Antonio feels pressured by his parents' claims on his destiny: "I know how hard it is to be in the middle when your parents try to decide your future. It is like you become an ant under the foot of your parents, waiting for them to step down." Serena told the story of her mother, who, more than anything, wanted her children to avoid the suffering she had faced as a sixteen-year-old mom and later the victim of physical abuse (which was witnessed by her children) at the hands of a boyfriend. Many of my students wrote that Antonio sees too much suffering and violence as a child, yet in their midst, sitting quietly, were many of their peers who had experienced intense suffering, fear, and loss. As Antonio was revealing his experiences, these quiet students started to tell their stories, too.

The intensity of Antonio's experiences permeates every element of the novel: his home, his family, his uncles' farm, his friendships, the town, the *llano*, his dreams, and especially the river. The river is the site of three deaths, the home of the Golden Carp, which some characters in the novel worship, the source of waters that could both flood and nourish, and the home of the bogeyman-like La Llorona (the crying woman). Repeatedly we read that the river has a *presence*, and the students constantly discussed what that presence might be, why the word *presence* is always italicized, and whether the river is enchanted. Emily wrote:

> Before reading this book, I never thought of a river as being evil. To me rivers always seemed to be places blossoming with life. Now I think of the turbulent waters of the river, brimming with restlessness and even an evil hunger. The river, although a vital source of fresh water, can lead you to your doom. I can relate this presence of the river with the dark. There is always a fear of darkness for fear of concealing secrets. A river can also conceal secrets; it is impossible to tell what is lying beneath the murky waters.

Anaya's book appeals to that part of us that loves fairy tales and magic, that imagines (or, for some, recognizes) a world where every living thing has breath and consciousness, a world very much alive in the Southwest today in the cultural traditions of various Native American groups, of the Mesoamerican folk culture, and, to some degree, even of environmentalists. As we read together, we admired how much respect the main characters show for the earth. When Ultima takes Antonio to gather the herbs that she uses for both food and medicine, she teaches him to thank the plant before harvesting it and to respect the taking of its life. My class found this ritual beautiful, and we talked about how much we take our own food—and its sources— for granted. In the novel, every character has a distinct connection to either the town or its natural surroundings, a connection that is often surprising. The most striking example is Narciso, the town drunk. Narciso is secretly a gardener of mystical success who creates an Eden-like sanctuary as a monument to the dead wife he mourns. The garden is verdant and resists, to an almost supernatural degree, the dryness of the surrounding *llano*. This secret and beautiful garden adds a sense of spiritual depth to Narciso and makes his sacrifice (he dies trying to save Ultima from the murderous Tenorio) and his dying confession to Antonio even more poignant. His death is not just the passing of a hero but also that of someone with a magical gift for fostering natural beauty and peace.

In the world Anaya creates, nature is a powerful presence, and humans are not masters but rather part of a unity.

> You both know [Ultima] spoke to my father and my mother, that the sweet water of the moon which falls as rain is the same water that gathers into rivers and flows to fill the seas. Without the waters of the moon to replenish the oceans there would be no oceans. And the same salt waters of the oceans are drawn by the sun to the heavens, and in turn become again the waters of the moon. Without the sun there would be no waters formed to slake the dark earth's thirst.

The waters are one, Antonio. I looked into her bright, clear
eyes and understood her truth.

You have been seeing the parts, she finished, and not looking
beyond into the great cycle that binds us all. (*Bless Me, Ultima*
[New York: Warner Books, 1994], 121)

The unity Ultima speaks of applies not just to the world and its
people but also to Antonio's family conflict. He feels bound to choose
between the way of his mother and the way of his father; here Ultima
offers a hint of resolution. Perhaps he can allow everyone he admires
and loves (as well as the town, the family farm, and the wide-open
llano) to be part of the unity that is Antonio. In class, this led to a hands-
on examination of the novel's connection to Jungian psychoanalysis.
Jung believed that every human psyche includes sun (conscious) and
shadow (subconscious) qualities that we represent symbolically in
stories, metaphors, and dreams. My class practiced this concept by
charting and drawing opposing nature symbols (including animals,
plants, minerals, and the weather) to represent the conscious and
subconscious aspects of personality. (You can find instructions for this
project in Fran Claggett and Joan Brown's *Drawing Your Own Con-
clusions.*) Each student's drawings fitted into a unifying circle ("mandala") that set all the symbols into a whole, and we could easily see how
Antonio, too, could be a blend of conflicting influences and forces.

The mandala project provided a framework for deeply understanding the connections forged by Anaya's use of animals and magical beings from folklore and myth (both traditional and invented
ones). Totem animals represented the human practitioners of magic—
an owl is a symbol of wisdom for the healer Ultima, and coyotes are
sly scavengers and traditional southwestern troublemakers for the evil
Trementina clan. Throughout our reading, my class speculated about
the involvement and nature of these animals. Are they only animals,
trained to assist their masters? Messengers (as in the current fantasy
favorite *Harry Potter*)? Are they magical? Connected to the soul of
their master or mistress? They present a suspenseful mystery to be

solved. We also encountered an evil, homicidal mermaid, who, like Homer's Sirens, lures men to their deaths. But the creature most disturbing to both Antonio and the reader is the Golden Carp.

The Golden Carp, an ancient secret kept by a small number of people in Antonio's town, is an oversize golden carp that can be seen only by those who are ready to believe. The Carp had once been a god but had then chosen to become a fish so he could take care of his people who, as punishment for their misdeeds, had been transformed into carp. When Antonio sees the Golden Carp, he feels that the creature is aware of him, too. This awareness gives the Carp an immediacy that the deity of his Catholic faith has so far lacked for him.

Marisa wrote:

> The Golden Carp seems like it is really God, but in a physical form that you are actually able to see. I, along with some other people, have a very hard time believing in God, because it's hard to believe in something that you can't see, feel, or smell. So I think that maybe this Golden Carp could be the boy's way of saying who God is because it is easier to believe in something that you can see.

The issue of faith isn't just Antonio's issue—it is Marisa's too. Later on she echoed some of Antonio's deepest confusion when she asked, "Why is it that innocent people get punished in the worst ways for doing absolutely nothing to deserve it?" This may be a fictional book based on folklore, dreams, magic, and one man's life, but its core issues and struggles are astonishingly vivid. Marisa's question is arrived at by all thoughtful people at some point in their lives, whether they are religious or not.

In class we talked about how psychologically powerful nature must be for people who believe that their god or gods are embedded in nature and aware of the people around them—a religion with neither church nor services. For some of my students, the perspective was new: around the world people practice or have practiced their religion in a great variety of ways that fall outside the conventions of mainstream faiths in the United States. Kyle wrote:

This passage really made me think about faith and god and whether or not there really is a "right" faith—if one specific religion is correct. If so, are the rest of the religions just wrong? This would mean millions of people get up every day praying, but because the premise of their religion is "wrong," then whoever is god just ignores them. No, I would find that hard to believe.

Kyle had used the novel as a jumping-off point to tap into a major theological, cultural, and even political issue. Antonio's crisis of faith is specific to his situation, family, and culture, yet it draws us into a consideration of truly universal real-life issues.

In *Bless Me, Ultima,* Antonio fears an apocalypse, a prophesied flood that will sweep away the sins of the town of Las Pasturas. His confusion about the definition of *sin* intensifies his fears. He is afraid that once he "loses his innocence," he will, by definition, be sinful. He has a child's desire for the world and the people he loves to be perfect. His struggle with the world's imperfections and with negotiating the presence of death, desire, and sin gave our class occasion to consider how we address the imperfections, crises, and darkness in our own environments. In the world of the novel, every character and event seem to have a shadow image that shows a different path, a different choice. Antonio's mother wants a stable life; his father longs for new adventures. Ultima uses magic to heal, and the Trementina sisters lay curses and malevolent spells. Antonio's growing awareness of these complexities and the intense means by which they are revealed in both his dreams and his reality create conflicts that many adults would be hard-pressed to handle. Thus, Antonio is, to my students, profoundly unsheltered. He witnesses several violent deaths. People he cares about have problems with alcohol. Men, including his brothers, return from the war changed, even psychologically damaged. He learns that his brothers spend their free time with prostitutes. He does not understand any of this, really, but since it surrounds him, he is forced to try.

The class responded to him as if he was a real person; they felt bad for him but also admired him for maintaining his goodness in the face of stress and disappointment. As we read, our own stories and memories bubbled out in our discussions and in writing.

As we read, I asked my students to look for passages in the novel that stood out for them as important, exceptionally well written, or steeped in meaning. My goal was to get each student to practice a close reading and literary analysis, which they did. But the greater impact, the true riches, came from the opportunity this journaling provided to explore issues of personal experience and philosophy. For example, Anaya writes, "Father says that the town steals our freedom." To this sentence, Jennifer responded,

> I realized that it was true; even in our Louisville the town steals our freedom. As I thought of what the author meant by freedom, I thought he wanted to show that in the town everyone is so [caught up] in the everyday rush that they lose their own personality. Everyone gets into the fashion trends and the cool places to hang out. You lose the freedom to be you because you are trying to be someone cooler and more popular.

Jennifer's town was nothing like Antonio's small rural community, but she found a piece of herself to analyze in her dialogue with the text—in the rest of her journal she came back numerous times to the theme of learning how to be an individual and fighting the pressures to conform blindly.

The journals also demonstrated visceral emotional responses to some events in the book. A number of students chose to react to a scene in which Antonio is made fun of at school for bringing a lunch made with tortillas instead of white bread. The students found this passage painful and the behavior of the other children unjust and cruel. In fact, the whole issue of being new at school and feeling like an outsider was still fresh in the minds of many ninth graders, and they wrote about it with great empathy for Antonio and for each other. Amy wrote:

> It must be hard being in a new building that looks really big, a building where you don't know where anything is and you

don't know anyone else there. The first day of school is always hard . . . ; it would be even worse if you didn't speak the language. And getting that feeling in your stomach that makes you feel like you're going to throw up. And knowing that you don't have anyone to go to because you don't know anyone to go to because you don't know anyone at the school and you don't know who speaks the same language as you.

Amy used her reading and writing to get into Antonio's head, to empathize and connect with his experiences based on what she knew from her own.

Bless Me, Ultima provided not only an abundance of questions to consider but also a model of a person (granted, a fictional one) actively engaging in self-examination. The weight of this seriousness did have a downside for a few readers. Some of my students did not like this book, mostly because "it was too philosophical," and they did not want to examine themselves or the ideas it brought up. A few complained that Antonio's childhood was too painful. In a way, these complaints are praise—Anaya succeeds in making the characters and situations vivid enough to make some readers uncomfortable. Great literature should make us squirm, question, debate, complain, and celebrate—its ability to evoke thoughtful or emotional responses is what makes it great. Like fire, it can illuminate, burn, and even pave the way for new growth.

But intense as it can be, *Bless Me, Ultima* also provided relief for us in moments of beauty, warmth, joy, and humor. The boys in the class especially recognized parts of themselves or their friends in Antonio's friends: Abel, Horse, Bones, the Vitamin Kid, and the rest. They loved the rituals of friendship and fighting, the weird rumors that spread, the pranks and transgressions.

In one of my favorite rituals in reading *Bless Me, Ultima* with a class, I read aloud to them, using my best storytelling acting, the funniest scene in the novel. (Actually, it is the funniest scene I've read in *any* novel.) Antonio and his friends arrive at school on the day of a huge snowstorm only to find that all the girls have been kept home for the day (and at this point we stopped briefly so that the girls in the class could speak their minds about the pros and cons of being a girl in the novel's town of Las Pasturas!). Their teacher, Miss Violet, decides that the boys should still go through with their plans to present a Nativity play to the entire school and should play all the parts. Anaya's humor draws on his great love for his characters and a fondness for the way children perceive and misperceive the trappings of both religion and theater. During the play, each of the boys comes into his full comic force. The profane, burly Horse is hilariously miscast as the Virgin Mary, the baby doll in the manger loses its head, and a full range of wonderfully described disasters and miscues take place. As I read to the class, I could barely control my laughter. Tears rolled out of my eyes as the scene reached its climax. We'd all been laughing during ten minutes of reading, with some of my students getting tears in their eyes too, when one of the guys yelled across the room, "Hey, Ms. K, can we act this part out as a play?" Another student came up after class and thanked me by saying, "I've been needing to laugh like that all week."

As real as much of the novel feels, Anaya always draws us back into the world of dreams and magic. Although the fantasy-filled dream sequences are clearly shown as symbolic operations of Antonio's unconscious mind, many of the magical, waking events are ambiguous. Clearly the narrator, Antonio, believes in magic. On his first day at school, he wants to ask his teacher "immediately about the magic in the letters" so he can learn to write his name. Of course, he learns that the letters are not literally magic, but in his world many other things are. Ultima's healing powers combine herbal lore and magical skill. The Trementina sisters are evil *brujas*, who use their magic to attack enemies that Anaya mentions. A belief in witches, curses, ghosts, and magical creatures is mentioned numerous times, and magical phenomena are accepted by all the characters as real. As Emily noted, "In *Bless Me, Ultima,* events containing magic are as ordinary or commonplace as any other event." This is the essential definition of magical realism, a literary technique popularized by Latin American authors such as Gabriel García Márquez and, in Chicano literature, by Anaya.

Emily went on to express a thought about this, noted by many other students in their own journals: "The idea of magical realism makes me remember being a child. When you are young, you believe almost everything. If someone told you that witches lived next door, you would give them the same credibility as if they had told you an old lady lived next door." Actually, quite a few of the students told me that the presence of magic is their favorite part of the book—the world of the unknown is inherently suspenseful and surprising. And as we shared our own memories of times when we all believed in magic as children, it was fascinating to notice how many students had arrived at the same fantastic explanations for common events or shared similar spooky experiences. Even the scary experiences were remembered with fondness.

Antonio's journey brought these teenagers back into their childhoods and allowed each student to reexamine his or her own early days. In addition, Antonio's struggles led my students to confront and further develop their own philosophies. Through reading, writing, and conversation, *Bless Me, Ultima* opened doors for my students and me, but not just into Anaya's fictional world. His powerful blend of myth and reality, of the spiritual and the worldly, exposed other doors, too, doors leading into different avenues of thinking about faith, school, family, growing up, love, loss, and courage. Readers willing to step through the doors will find the journey worthwhile.

• SPIRITUAL JOURNEYS •

Hesse, Hermann,   *Siddhartha,* 144
Hulme, Keri,   *The Bone People,* 146
Márquez, Gabriel García,   *One Hundred Years of Solitude,* 156
Naylor, Gloria,   *Mama Day,* 160
Neruda, Pablo,   *Selected Poems,* 161
Robbins, Tom,   *Even Cowgirls Get the Blues,* 166
Robbins, Tom,   *Skinny Legs and All,* 166
Sagan, Carl,   *Contact,* 168
Silko, Leslie Marmon,   *Ceremony,* 171
Storm, Hyemeyohsts,   *Seven Arrows,* 172

• FATHERS AND SONS •

Agee, James,   *A Death in the Family,* 119
Anaya, Rudolfo,   *Bless Me, Ultima,* 78
Banks, Russell,   *Rule of the Bone,* 125
Castillo, Anna,   *So Far from God,* 128
Diamant, Anita,   *The Red Tent,* 131
Kesey, Ken,   *Sometimes a Great Notion,* 150
Maclean, Norman,   *A River Runs through It*
   and Other Stories, 154

Maraire, J. Nozipo,   *Zenzele,* 155
Spiegelman, Art,   *Maus,* 171
Steinbeck, John,   *East of Eden,* 171

CULTURE AND SURVIVAL

Sherman Alexie's *Reservation Blues*

~

Sarah Talbot

I AM SITTING WITH MY group of twelve students in a public school classroom studying cross-cultural literature, my dream class; and we are reading Sherman Alexie's *Reservation Blues*, one of my favorite American novels. The students have chosen this novel, and the class is an elective. They are seniors learning in the winter before spring steals their brains, and can you imagine how lucky I feel? It's a Thursday, and I'm running a seminar in the way that I dreamed I would if only I had a small group of interested students who had some background in literature.

In *Reservation Blues* Thomas Builds-the-Fire, a quirky storyteller turned musician, grapples with his seemingly incompatible needs to connect tribally on the reservation and to survive the results of racist oppression specifically targeted at the reservation. Alexie examines the ways in which Reservation Indians support each other in the face of colonized America by exploring Thomas's obsessive attraction to the bullies Junior Polatkin and Victor Joseph (who, in an ironic juxtaposition with his historic name, fights forever). Big Mom, a goddess figure, steps out of time and space in one moment, then wins big at Bingo the next; she connects the narrative and the characters to the spiritual Pandora's box of Native history. In the end, she acts as a witness when Thomas loses everything but love and stories and leaves the reservation.

These are the important themes, but not the real reason I offered the kids a chance to read this book. I chose it because it's funny. I hoped my students would be able to connect with Alexie's dark humor, his flippant references to an Indian culture that has been saved, found, stolen, and reinvented. After all, they spend each day walking in their segregated teenage world, fighting powerlessness in the face of an unchecked authority. I happen to *be* that authority, at least in their minds, but I hoped Alexie could help them work around me. My students rediscover their power and their powerlessness each day in classrooms and in their homes; they negotiate a grade, introduce me to a new idea, and get detention for asserting themselves at inconvenient times. They understand what it means to feel so hopeless that you have to laugh. They understand what it means to be misunderstood, and I hoped that would lead them through *Reservation Blues;* after all, high school blues can't be much different, can it?

It turned out to be more complicated. First, since Native American culture is so little understood in dominant American culture, it is not surprising that Alexie's intentions weren't immediately clear to my students. "'The end of the world is near!' shouted the crazy old Indian man in front of the Spokane Tribal Trading Post. He wasn't a Spokane Indian, but nobody knew what tribe he was." Throughout the rest of the novel this character is referred to as The-Man-Who-Was-Probably-Lakota, and kids could relate to him. They joked in class about "That-Freshman-with-the-Purple-Mohawk" and how everybody knew who that was, but none of them knew his name or where he was from. Still, they missed poking soft fun at Indian names; they didn't know if people really do get names like Dances with Wolves, and they jokingly started naming each other. Their knowledge was so shallow, with only Kevin Costner and Sherman Alexie to draw understanding from, that they didn't get that part of the joke.

Later, Alexie aims his comic cannon at the cultural flexibility of time:

"We thought we was two hours late by real time. At least an hour late by Indian time."

"Shit, people out here work on double Indian time. You could've showed up tomorrow and been okay."

I thought they might talk about time in their families, whether being on time meant arriving ten minutes before the stated time, as it did to my mother, or half an hour after, as it did to my aunt. For some reason they didn't get this; perhaps the regimens of school had replaced their cultural understandings of time.

Alexie approaches the tender heart of Indian alcoholism with gentle, sweet humor. Each character in the novel is affected by alcoholism—either his or her own or a parent's. Chess and Checkers Warm Water imagine their father's attention restored from the numbing effects of alcohol.

> Chess and Checkers pulled off their shoes and tiptoed into their dad's room, which stank of whisky and body odor. Luke Warm Water slept alone and dreamed of his missing wife.
>
> "Hey Dad," Chess whispered. "We're going to church. Is that okay?"
>
> Luke snored.
>
> "Good. I'm glad you agree. Do you want to come this time?"
>
> Luke snored.
>
> "I don't think it's a good idea, either. Maybe next time?"
>
> Luke snored.
>
> "Don't get mad at me. Jeez. If you walked into church, everybody might die of shock."
>
> "Yeah," Checkers said. "The whole roof might fall down."

This scene always makes me want to cry, then laugh. The tragic vision of two little girls readying for church while their dad sleeps off the previous night's drunkenness didn't appeal to my students' capacities for empathy, but the Warm Waters' bravado in the face of a sleeping authority did. They laughed at the girls' sassiness to their father because they could relate to it. Each of them had brave words for a teacher or a parent when the adult couldn't hear them, but none of them knew *quite* what to do with Luke's failure as a parent. Maybe their age prevented them from relating to his utter despair and thus connecting with him in the scene.

But the dynamic went further than just missing cues. It's such a funny, funny book. I knew they would love it, and they did. I just didn't know they would use Alexie's humor to reaffirm their own stereotypes. Seated in a large circle discussing the text, looking up quotes, and clarifying the plot and characters' names, they start talking about the humor Alexie uses to discuss the difficult issues his book brings up, and the conversation goes to a place I didn't anticipate.

"Why are there even reservations?"

"Don't Indians have special privileges?"

"Yeah, don't they get money from the government?"

"If they hate the reservations so much, if the reservations are so bad, why don't they just leave?"

"Yeah, can't they go to college for free?"

"Why are all these Indians so poor?"

"Why do they kill whales? Aren't they endangered?"

"Why are they all alcoholics?"

"How come they can take as many fish as they want, even endangered species?"

"Aren't all Indians alcoholics? Isn't it genetic or something?"

The stereotypes they articulated were, in a complicated way, half reinforced by the way they were reading this novel, a novel I thought was indisputably pro-Indian, pro-reservation, and beautiful. How did the misreading happen? How could it be turned around?

I normally teach a class of thirty students from backgrounds as diverse as public schools allow, and many students walk into my classes with racist assumptions. But these twelve students, ten of whom were upper-middle-class white kids with liberal parents, had seemed different. They seemed more mature, ready to spring out into the world, and they'd had my class for some time. I'd been working with these students for six months, and I liked them. I'd grown to love Yen's rare smiles and carefully controlled body movements. I was amused by

Adam's lankiness when he slumped in his favorite chair (the one with wheels) right before he got excited by a discussion with Annie and Randy about toaster pastries. Kathy's quiet reading and insightful observations had become a part of my day that I looked forward to. But now they were asking what I heard as racist questions, and I felt betrayed. I wanted to focus on the literature, the words and the jokes themselves—the joy of Alexie's facile linguistic dance. I wanted to share things about this book that I love. And I couldn't.

But when I look back, how could I expect Randy to interpret Lester Falls Apart's taunting of Officer Wilson on page 102 (New York: Warner Books, 1995)?

> "You two been drinking?"
> "I've been drinking since I was five," Lester said. "Kinder-garten is hard on a man."

I was rolling on the floor when I first read this line. I thought that any teenager would relate to smart-mouthing a police officer. But could Randy understand that Alexie is playing with racial stereotypes *and* characterizing Lester as an alcoholic? Could he understand a humor that goes beyond the absurd notion of a five-year-old drinking after kindergarten and into the painful truth of Native alcoholism? He didn't. He wondered how Indians could be such bad parents that they let their children drink in elementary school. He did get that Lester was teasing the cop, but he didn't get the joke. In the first seminar, he read that passage as evidence that all Native people are alcoholics.

What about Yen, our drill leader? She'd taken the hardest classes my school had to offer, but how could she leave behind her reality as a Vietnamese immigrant and enter American popular culture enough to connect with passages like the following one? "Coyote Springs created a tribal music that scared and excited the white people in the audience. That music might have chased away the pilgrims five hundred years ago. But if they were forced, Indians would have adopted the ancestors of a few whites like Janis Joplin's great-great-great-great-grandparents, and let them stay in America." Even if Yen figured out who Janis Joplin was, how could she connect to the feeling of being invaded by immigrants? Wouldn't it just alienate her? How could she help but feel more defensive, especially given the anti-immigrant sentiments of some members of our community? In class she sounded confused, questioning why the characters complain so much and why they haven't "made it" in America, where she sees that hard work can lead to success.

Adam's single mom took him to church every Sunday, and he worked hard for good grades. Nothing came easily to him. He washed dishes, sometimes until two in the morning, to pay for his car insurance and buy the clothes his mother couldn't afford. After reading about Junior's tragedies, how could he forgive his suicide? "Everybody on the Spokane Indian Reservation had heard the rumors, but nobody had known the truth except Junior. After Junior killed himself, Victor found that note in Junior's wallet and learned the whole story. Lynn, the little romance, the abortion." Adam couldn't connect with the tragedy of Junior's loneliness. He called Junior damned to hell.

My personality and background perhaps created as much of an impediment as the students' did. I'm white—I carry white privilege in a big ol' bag on my back—and have Indian family members. My children's grandmother on their dad's side and my grandfather were both Bureau Indians; neither was a member of her or his tribe, but both were recognized by the federal government as racially Native and carriers of BIA (Bureau of Indian Affairs) cards. My grandfather did not hold white privilege, and something about his vision of the world peers through my blue eyes. My kids' grandmother is a big part of my life, and we talk about Native issues fairly often, particularly about whether she will try to join and sign my children up with the tribe from which she descended. Maybe it was these conversations that made me believe that everyone understands Native issues. Maybe it was my experiences at the Evergreen State College, where Native American Studies has long been a cornerstone of the curriculum. But somewhere, somehow, I forgot that most people don't have much of an intellectual focal point for understanding Native cultures.

And Alexie's skill at drawing characters that are at once completely rooted and universal made me forget that the universality might not be immediately apparent to some readers. I felt that everyone, in every culture, was familiar with these characters. I thought every social group had a storyteller like Thomas, who never shut up, who made everyone groan. I thought every father wore the silent reticence of Victor and the honesty of Junior. The characters touched me close to my experience, though I am white, though I grew up working class, though I never even drove across the Spokane Reservation.

I sputtered through the end of that first crushing Thursday seminar, confused about how to separate the students from their stereotypes in a respectful way, but compelled to do so. I shut up after I found myself talking after each kid and defending the characters and—unbelievable to me now—all Native people. When I began to sound like a liberal textbook, I finally clamped my jaw and swallowed my tongue.

At home that night I fumed until my partner asked me, "How many Native people do your kids know?"

"It sounds like none," I had to admit, though our school has a small number of tribally enrolled Native students.

"Where did they get these ideas about Native people?"

"I guess from the media—the news, movies."

"How many of them have seen a movie with Native American people in it?"

"I guess half of them may have seen *Smoke Signals*," I answered. It struck me that Alexie's wolfish humor was the only fiction they'd ever seen from a Native perspective. They didn't understand the novel's irony because they had no connection to the context, and irony out of context makes no sense. They couldn't hang Alexie's metaphorical shorthand—government applesauce, epic basketball games, characters named after board games—on any experiences, and metaphor robbed of its physicality becomes surreal and confusing.

I decided to stop being irritated and outraged with what my students failed to know and to try my best to teach it.

On Friday I came armed to class with a list of all the larger topics the students had expressed preconceived notions about: tribal sovereignty, federal benefits, fishing rights, alcoholism, poverty rates, and BIA boarding schools. I divided the class into groups of two or three, and each group hopped onto one of our school's computers to learn.

Ten years ago, I would have had to go to our state library and retrieve data from a variety of sources to hand over to kids, and even then they would have had to take my word that the sources were unbiased. On that day, the groups found at least three Web sites from credible sources, showing a broad range of perspectives on their topic. As students were researching, I wandered the room. I questioned the credibility of their sources and listened to them defend it. We brainstormed key words together. I helped them find federal and tribal definitions and data. I asked them probing questions about their work; when one group found that there was a genetic link between alcoholism and certain races, I asked them whether that meant Natives were predisposed to it. They found that it did not. When one group found a simplistic definition of *sovereignty,* I asked why Native people sometimes end up in federal prisons. When one kid became obsessed with Makah whaling, I asked why East Coast tribes don't whale. I bugged and probed and pushed them to deeply understand one big contextual idea that would give them access to the novel.

On Monday I found out that the kids had looked for information over the weekend—without being asked! They finished their searches in class and began to put together presentations explaining what they'd found out and where they'd found it. The presentations were solid, but not half as eloquent as the look on Yen's face as she explained why so many Native people live in poverty. She could understand what it would mean to leave one's homeland; she saw how Thomas struggled over whether to leave the reservation, the only place on the planet where his culture was preserved. Yen had watched as her parents struggled to abandon a small farm in Vietnam, where they had to leave behind a community that understood them. Randy summarized research showing that many Native Americans and Chinese people lack genetic protection against alcoholism, which is connected to a sensitivity to wheat products. Adam gave a moving account of Bureau Indian schools, which kidnapped children, kept them away from their families, and forced them to abandon their cultures. They presented the information with their brains standing a few feet away from the racism of Thursday's seminar. They gave each other a little bit of the context that lies behind Alexie's irony.

∼

Thursday rolled around again, and the seminar opened with a different set of questions:

"What would have saved Victor and Junior?"

"Is Big Mom God? How can they be Christians and go to the church and still all believe in these powers that Big Mom supposedly has?"

"Why can't the devil come onto the reservation after Robert Johnson, or after the guitar once Victor has it?"

"Why does Junior put up with Victor? Why do they like each other so much?"

"Why does everybody hate Thomas's stories? Why does he keep telling them?"

"Why is Chess obsessed with father figures? Why isn't she obsessed with mothers?"

"Why do you think Alexie uses the symbol of the screaming horses? What does that mean to the Spokane tribe?"

I felt the relief like a miracle. They had begun to see the novel as a novel—to contextualize the experiences of the characters just enough to be able to ask questions about the novel, its structure, and its use of literary figures. Our conversation progressed, not without misguided comments, but without the two-dimensionality of the previous week's conversation. With a little more background, more engagement on their own with the larger context, my students had finally come to see some of the brilliant complexity Alexie lets us in on.

I wanted to push them a little further, too. I wanted to show how their prejudices affected their reading and kept them from understanding Alexie's humorous exploration of tragedy. I didn't want to confront them in the way I had been confronted about my internalized racism in difficult classes in college. They weren't out looking for antiracist teaching and learning, as I had been. They just wanted to read good books. But I wanted to show that you have to be able to move beyond your own racism in order to understand what's good about those books.

So after doing our regular character analysis workshop on Friday, I took on the concept—theirs and mine—that racism is something that used to happen. Instead of trying to scare them or accuse them, I presented my lesson as if it were about my own learning. I went to the Web site for the Southern Poverty Law Center during my prep period and took several of the tests that show unconscious bias. When my students came to class (they see me during the sixth period, directly after my prep), they found me scowling at the screen, playing what to them looked like a game.

"You guys have to check this out," I said as Kathy and Adam sauntered in.

"What is it?" they asked. As the rest of the students filed in, I ranted and raved about how I'd been taking these tests, and now I was trying to fool the program to see if it could be trusted. I told them that the results of the first test I'd taken showed I had an unconscious association between African Americans and weapons. Then I wrote the URL of the Web site on the board. We spent the rest of the period taking bias tests, including one that tries to detect whether subjects unconsciously associate Native American or white American faces with the word *foreign*. Everybody but Annie found that they had an unconscious bias. Some students questioned whether the measure could be trusted, and I told them I had failed to fool it when I had tried. I lectured the class briefly, explaining how we develop unconscious biases, how they aren't really about what we believe in our conscious minds but rather how well we've filtered and eventually accepted the racist messages we see every day. Randy later reflected, "This [the bias test] changed the way I think. . . . After taking the tests, I now know that despite my conscience nonprejudice [*sic*] beliefs, I have some prejudices that are built in by society."

〜

Teaching this class didn't eliminate my students' misunderstandings. It only gently moved them away from the assumptions with which they had walked into the room. Randy grappled unsuccessfully with the numbers of alcoholics, assuming that there are more Native American alcoholics than white ones, even though Native Americans are a small minority. Kathy wondered whether the narrator hates white people; Adam imagined the narrator as a born-again Christian (a characterization I'm sure Alexie would find amusing).

But nobody asked why Native people stay on reservations. None of my students asked Alexie if he was an alcoholic. No one asked about fishing rights. We did learn something significant.

And they loved the book. Of the twelve students, nine said it was their favorite book of the term. Kathy wrote in her final, "Thomas, Chess, and Checkers leave the home of their people, but because they take a knowledge of themselves and their cultural history, they are able to attain personal freedom." Through this novel, she came to understand a beautiful concept. Everyone found something to connect with.

The students had to unlearn only a little bit to connect with the characters, to love and cheer for Thomas's stories and cry at Junior's and Victor's deaths. The book does connect universally. Although Yen never really understood the context of the Spokane's poverty, she overcame her defensiveness and connected with Thomas, Chess, and Checkers, who move away from their homes but hope to hold tight to their cultures. Adam couldn't like a narrator who wasn't Christian, so he imagined Alexie as Christ-like, making his peace with a religion that he recognized violated the Spokane's humanity. The students never rid themselves completely of prejudice, but the preconceptions that kept them from initially respecting and responding to this novel weakened. The book worked its magic, wove its story under their old ideas, and began to grow new ones for them. I only had to create an opening.

• HISTORY REIMAGINED •

Alexie, Sherman,	*Reservation Blues*, 91
Baldwin, James,	*Notes of a Native Son*, 124
Chevalier, Tracy,	*Girl with a Pearl Earring*, 129
Galeano, Eduardo,	*Memory of Fire* (trilogy), 138
O'Brian, Patrick,	*Master and Commander*, 162
Twain, Mark,	*The Mysterious Stranger and Other Stories*, 175
Walker, Margaret,	*Jubilee*, 177
Williams, John A.,	*The Man Who Cried I Am*, 178
Yoshikawa, Eiji,	*Musashi*, 181

• GOTTA LAUGH TO KEEP FROM CRYING •

Alexie, Sherman,	*Ten Little Indians*, 120
Bambara, Toni Cade,	*Gorilla, My Love*, 124
Eggers, Dave,	*A Heartbreaking Work of Staggering Genius*, 133
Gogol, Nicolai,	*Dead Souls*, 139
Heller, Joseph,	*Catch-22*, 143
Himes, Chester,	*Cotton Comes to Harlem*, 145
Himes, Chester,	*Yesterday Will Make You Cry*, 145
Hornby, Nick,	*High Fidelity*, 145
Irving, John,	*The Hotel New Hampshire*, 146
Irving, John,	*A Prayer for Owen Meany*, 146
Irving, John,	*The World According to Garp*, 146
Ives, David,	*All in the Timing*, 147
Kesey, Ken,	*One Flew Over the Cuckoo's Nest*, 150
Kosinski, Jerzy N.,	*Being There*, 151
Nichols, John Treadwell,	*Milagro Beanfield War*, 161
Robbins, Tom,	*Skinny Legs and All*, 166
Sedaris, David,	*Me Talk Pretty One Day*, 169
Toole, John Kennedy,	*A Confederacy of Dunces*, 174

• CULTURAL SURVIVAL •

TRUE WAR STORIES: HOW DO YOU KNOW WHAT HAPPENED IF ALL YOU DID WAS SEE IT?

Tim O'Brien's *The Things They Carried*

~

Lauren Jackson and Alan James

W HEN WE BEGAN TEACHING the interdisciplinary American Studies course together at Hong Kong International School—a history teacher and literature teacher working together—we decided to focus on the question of historical perspective. "Who writes history? How is history affected by the writer's perspective?" We read an excerpt of Columbus's diary, the first chapter of Howard Zinn's *A People's History of the United States*, and Sherman Alexie's stories of Indian life in *The Lone Ranger and Tonto Fistfight in Heaven*. Each of these offered dramatically different views of Europeans' motives for their "invasion" of the New World and its long-term effects. After these long conversations about truth and perspective, then, our students knew what kind of questions we were asking. We opened the final unit about America at war in the twentieth century with the question: What is the truth about Vietnam?

This is, of course, a loaded question for anyone American. It carries connotations and associations for Americans that our students in Hong Kong don't necessarily know. Not all of them identify with America. Although seventy-five percent of them carry U.S. passports, many have never lived in the United States or been a part of the American school system. At the same time, many students have traveled to Vietnam with their families, mostly to the unreal world of resorts. Thus they can picture Vietnam, its jungles and beaches, and they know where it is on the map. The school's Interim program (consisting of overseas travel for the entire school, for adventure, service, and culture) includes several service trips to Vietnam, mainly to orphanages, where students learn more about the country and its people. Some of our students, not so invested in America's being right, may be more open to multiple answers to the question about Vietnam. Recent transfers from local schools, however, with their distinctly Chinese "teacher knows all" approach, sometimes have a hard time believing that there isn't just one answer to a question. Nevertheless, they, like all students, are deeply concerned about truth.

• THE THINGS WE CARRY •

When we passed out Tim O'Brien's *The Things They Carried,* we read as much as we could of the first story, "The Things They Carried," out loud to the students. We took turns reading sections, Lauren reading those which deal with love and Alan those concerning supplies and weapons. When we divided the text in preparation for our reading, we were amazed to find how rhythmically O'Brien shifts back and forth between "He remembered kissing her goodnight at the dorm door" (*The Things They Carried* [New York: Broadway Books, 1998], 6) and "M-16 maintenance gear—rods and steel brushes and swabs and tubes of LSA oil" (7). At the same time, the two voices bleed into each other. In the paragraph with the M-60, M-16, and M-79, when they describe Lavender's death—"the poor bastard just flat-fuck fell. Boom. Down. Nothing else"—the lieutenant "pictured Martha's smooth young face, thinking he loved her more than anything" (7–8). And even in the first paragraph, O'Brien invokes and makes a problem out of the idea of truth. Lt. Jimmy Cross holds the letters from Martha, his schoolboy crush, and spends "the last hour of light pretending . . . imagining romantic camping trips into the White Mountains" (3). Immediately, we don't know what really happened between Cross and Martha. Just like Jimmy, we don't know what she means when she signs her letter "Love, Martha. . . . Love was only a way of signing and did not mean what he sometimes pretended it meant" (3–4).

When we finished the story and looked back at all the items the men are carrying, we knew they would stagger under the accumulated weight (just as the lieutenant staggers under his "cross," the burden of his responsibility for the men under him). Carrying all those things would be humanly impossible, but perhaps that's O'Brien's point.

> The things they carried were largely determined by necessity. Among the necessities or near-necessities were P-38 can openers, pocket knives, heat tabs, wristwatches, dog tags, mosquito repellent, chewing gum, candy, cigarettes, salt tablets, packets of Kool-Aid, lighters, matches, sewing kits, Military Payment Certificates, C rations, and two or three canteens of water. Together, these items weighed between 15 and 20 pounds, depending upon a man's habits or rate of metabolism. (2)

In any case, the students were caught up in the story. They heard O'Brien's powerful language read out loud, his lists and rhythms, and his military jargon, and they heard their teachers swear for the first time. The style seemed tediously repetitive to some students, who saw only dozens of unfamiliar or mundane objects listed one after another. Some were more drawn to O'Brien's reflective moments, when he pauses over a photo, one of the hundreds of things he carries: "She wore white gym shorts. Her legs, he thought, were almost certainly the legs of a virgin, dry and without hair, the left knee cocked and carrying her entire weight, which was just over 100 pounds" (4). O'Brien seems obsessed with the weight of objects, the precise labeling of items, the pounding cadence of lists. Mesmerized, the students nearly missed those delightful moments when O'Brien slips quietly from the physical to the metaphoric and back: "They shared the weight of memory.

They took up what others could no longer bear. Often, they carried each other, the wounded or weak" (14).

When we gave the students an essay-writing assignment called "The Things I Carry," the trick, then, was to get students simply to plunge in—to write about the things they carried in their pockets, on their backs—and to insist on precise detail. "But what brand of cell phone? Color? Latest model?" Initially students struggled with finding a balance between the physical and the metaphysical. For some of them, the first draft was little more than a list, with a final sentence that made some oblique reference to their inner struggle. Others wanted to skip over the list and jump right into baring their souls, telling us all that weighed them down. Candace wrote:

> She also always keeps her expensive TI-83 calculator in her bag, as she lost it many times before from misplacing it. She also carries her lunch—her favorite—a tomato, lettuce, and turkey sandwich; it's been one year and she still isn't sick of them. In the minipocket of her bag she carries her snacks, which usually is something healthy, like dried raisins or cut apples. She never keeps these foods in her locker because she had a disgusting encounter with ants the year before. She carries stress and fatigue from almost never-ending work, which is obvious from the black bags she carries under her eyes.

We tried a "read-around," in which students chose a place in their writing they were most proud of, a passage they wanted others to hear. Success was audible, palpable in the room, as polite silence was broken by spontaneous smiles or nodding heads.

"I carried Derek's humor on my way up and Fouad's humor on my way down."

"Pictures of my friends, because I don't know if I'll have them next year."

"A TI-83 Plus graphing calculator, capable of solving mathematical problems the human brain cannot, and a black Muji pencil case with a variety of Muji pencils and Muji pens for solving problems the calculator simply cannot."

"The first is a Kodacolor snapshot of a baby I nurtured in Mongolia; I am a victim of his smile."

A year later we still associate certain students with what they wrote in this assignment. Elizabeth lamented her "capacity for great empathy, yet an inability to console." Anthony, an atypically blithe spirit who fearlessly flouted our assignments when the opportunity to amuse and abuse classmates arose, wrote: "Candace kept peace with an Acu-Tek neural paralyzing rifle that shot rounds with a range of 8om, the length of around thirteen classrooms." These bursts of wit helped us tolerate his otherwise inattentive and disruptive behavior. Lauren was homesick as she wrote wistfully of carrying "buckeye from the valley of Cataloochi." In one of those classes, Stuart Lu read, "My paternal grandfather carried Camel cigarettes in his mouth. Even at breakfast. The left half of his lips clung to the Camel's filter and the right half drank coffee. He carried pieces of breakfast at the right corner of his mouth until he died. Cancer ate him up from the inside, starting from the bladder. You'd think the cigarettes killed him, but he got it in the pisser." The rest of the class was silent, caught up in the things Stuart's family carried and in his powerful writing. Six months later, the next school year, Stuart and I talked about this piece, and he told me that he didn't know what his Chinese parents would do to him if they read the essay, with its lack of filial piety and harsh criticisms. Somehow, Stuart had written a truth about his family that might never have been told by the others. They may not even have recognized it as truth. But it was Stuart's truth, it was the "story truth" (in O'Brien's words), and that's what mattered.

• DISCOVERING *THINGS* •

Much like Kurt Vonnegut in *Slaughterhouse-Five*, O'Brien aims to deal with life's truths through war stories. His final story, "The Lives of the Dead," is not so much about war as about the death of a little girl named Linda and how people deal with death. O'Brien opens it with the words "But this too is true: stories can save us" (256). He tells us that "even as a nine-year-old I had begun to practice the magic of stories. Some I just dreamed up. Others I wrote down—the scenes and dialogue" (272). In his stories as a nine-year-old, Linda comes alive again. Even the dead Linda knows the power of stories. She says that being dead is like being "inside a book that nobody's reading" (273). Though the Linda that the forty-three-year-old author writes about is "mostly made up" (273), none of that matters. The truth is there in the story, and the stories, the imagination, will save our lives. People need to tell stories to come to grips with experience, especially the experience of death.

O'Brien weaves these ideas all through the stories of *The Things They Carried*, so that they become more like chapters in a novel than stories in a book of short stories. We have even had debates about whether to call it a novel or a book of stories. It certainly hangs together as a literary text, and we can follow the themes, characters, and symbols all the way through it, as one would with a novel. In "Speaking of Courage," the character Norman Bowker, at home in Minnesota after the war, had no one to listen to his stories. In the next story, "Notes," O'Brien tells us that Bowker hanged himself. When he compares Bowker with himself, he realizes that the stories have saved him.

> By telling stories, you objectify your own experience. You separate it from yourself. You pin down certain truths. You make up others. You start sometimes with an incident that truly happened, like the night in the shit field, and you carry it forward by inventing incidents that did not in fact occur but that nonetheless help to clarify and explain. (179–80)

And yet Alan was skeptical of *The Things They Carried* as a valuable tool for learning the history associated with the Vietnam conflict. O'Brien, the Vietnam veteran, the primary source, the eyewitness to the war, proceeds to *invent* the very details of his experience in Vietnam. Alan was already accustomed to dismissing such films as *The Deer Hunter* as having no claim to truth. But at least the director of the movie seems to acknowledge his ignorance and includes no more than four minutes of combat footage. O'Brien was there, in Vietnam.

Why would the proverbial horse's mouth deliberately choose to make so much of his stories up?

And yet intuitively history teachers know that history is more than the accumulation of events and dates, but the sea of detail often drowns both students and teachers. Stories bring us back to the underlying currents of history—and those who write such stories evoke the time period in ways that speak to us all. And it's O'Brien's transparent acknowledgment that he is using invented stories to get at the real truth that ultimately wins us over, teachers and students alike.

• DEALING WITH TRUTH IN "HOW TO TELL A TRUE WAR STORY" •

Initially, after reading what O'Brien says about the truth of his stories, many students came back to class with a cheated feeling: "He never tells us what's really true. He contradicts himself. He's playing with us." O'Brien *sounds* so sincere, and then he throws it all into question, so that you can't trust anything he says anymore.

In trying to get students to think about these ideas of truth, both war truth and writing truth, we looked carefully at "How to Tell a True War Story." We asked them to write first: what does O'Brien say about truth? The students started reading closely on their own. The first quotation Anna read was: "In war you lose your sense of the definite, hence your sense of truth itself, and therefore it's safe to say that in a true war story nothing is ever absolutely true" (88).

"Yeah," Jen jumped in. "Things 'seem' because it's hard to know what really happened." Jen found a passage that matched Anna's: "In any war story, but especially a true one, it's difficult to separate what happened from what seemed to happen. What seems to happen becomes its own happening and has to be told that way" (78). "You have to tell it as it seems," she said, "as *you* felt it to be, or it's not true."

Alan reminded them, "Military communiqués and personal accounts often differ. Soldiers may start to doubt their own memories, their points of view." Earlier that week we had read Bob Kerry's story of the incident at Thanh Phong in *Time* magazine. The story was just breaking that month. Kerry's story and Gerhard Klann's were completely different. Kerry claimed that the shooting of the civilians was a horrible accident that happened while they were returning enemy fire. Klann said Kerry rounded up unarmed women and children and ordered his men to shoot them. We grappled with how the stories could be so different even though both men had been there. We also read a *New York Times* editorial by another Vietnam vet, Tobias Wolff. In his article entitled "War and Memory," Wolff writes, "We tend to think of memory as a camera . . . where the past can be filed intact. . . . But memory is a storyteller, and like all storytellers it imposes form on the raw mass of experience." Wolff conjectures that each man believes the story his memory has been telling him, although "witnesses to crimes and accidents are notoriously unreliable; imagine being young and terrified on a foggy night in enemy territory, everything going wrong, everything happening too fast. How could you see it clearly even at the time?" By that point, the students were starting to use O'Brien's arguments as their own. They nodded in agreement with Wolff. Liz concluded, "So the truth is *your* truth; it's what *you* see and remember."

Students also noticed some of the other philosophical issues O'Brien raises in "How to Tell a True War Story." Anthony gave us this quotation: "A true war story is never moral. It does not instruct, nor encourage virtue, nor suggest models of proper human behavior" (76). He wanted to know, "Is it the same thing to say that a story doesn't have a moral and that a story isn't moral?" We talked about the crude bluntness in parts of O'Brien's stories, about the sad cruelty, and about the foul language proving O'Brien's point that "There is no virtue." And when we read O'Brien's sentence "If at the end of a war story you feel uplifted . . . then you have been made the victim of a very old and terrible lie" (76), we couldn't resist making a connection to Wilfred Owen's lines, which they'd read a year earlier: "My friend, you would not tell with such high zest / To children ardent for some desperate glory, / The old Lie: Dulce et decorum est / Pro patria mori."

• THE VIETNAMESE IN *THINGS* •

With our commitment to multiple perspectives in American Studies, drawing from both documentary and literary sources, we could see that the story of the Vietnam War would not be complete without an examination of the Vietnamese themselves. How does O'Brien portray the "enemy"? Has he done a better job than all the other one-sided American stories about the war that we've seen in films?

The students looked closely at "The Man I Killed," one of O'Brien's attempts to include the Vietnamese perspective. "The man I killed . . . had been born, maybe, in 1946 in the village of My Khe near the central coastline of Quang Ngai Province, where his parents farmed" (125). The details are extensive. We learn about a delicate young soldier, newly wed, a mathematics scholar who sees poetry in numbers, whose life is blown from his body in a nearly soundless explosion by the hand of the grief-stricken author. "No sweat, man, what else could you do?" asks O'Brien's buddy, Kiowa. "Tim, this is a war. The guy wasn't Heidi—he had a weapon, right? (126). After one reading, the students were drawn to the anguish of death—they felt O'Brien's pain, his remorse—they could see the mangled Vietnamese soldier. O'Brien describes in chilling detail the devastation he caused: "The upper lip and gum and teeth were gone. The man's head was cocked at a wrong angle, as if loose at the neck, and the neck was wet with blood" (126). This is the stuff of modern war movies—not the clean deaths of soldiers in pre-1990s war films—this is the slow-knife-in-the-chest of a *Saving Private Ryan* or a bayonet charge in *Glory*. But even better, this is a Vietnamese soldier—even *Platoon* or the much-hyped *We Were Soldiers* doesn't give viewers real people for enemies. The named actors are on our side, and in 1990s films they die horribly, gloriously, but the enemy soldiers still always die quickly and in droves. Here at last was our chance to discuss the Vietnamese perspective on the war, who the soldiers were as people, and how an American soldier might have felt when he came face to face with his enemy and realized that the man he had killed didn't want to be there all.

The classroom conversation started with just the right tone. Predictably, the opening comments dealt with the gore, the vision of death, and O'Brien's shell shock from what he had done. "How would you feel if you had killed someone? Would you, like O'Brien later tells us, cover it up, refuse to admit to your own children that you actually wasted someone in war?" The students for the most part didn't think so; they were still too used to movie wars to be drawn in. They admitted that O'Brien's grief seems real, but they tended to side with Kiowa, who said, "Stop *staring*." "Five minutes, Tim. Five more minutes and we're moving out" (129). Anthony, our bluntest student, stated, "If it were my job to kill someone in war, I'd just do it." But we challenged the kids here: "What if you knew something about the man you killed? Knew a lot about him, in fact, and realized that that guy was recently married, was forced to join the war effort by his circumstances, and was far more scared than you? If you knew all that before you fired, would you shoot?" The discussion was getting stickier. "But you wouldn't know, you couldn't know, could you?" "Just pretend you could. There were cases of this in the Civil War, when family members or people from the same town met on the battlefield. Is it so far-fetched to imagine looking the other way? Aiming high?" "Right, but those were people from the same country—we're talking about Vietnamese and American soldiers here. It can't be the same." So then why does Tim O'Brien pretend that he does know this man? Why does he make up such an elaborate and touching story? Is he trying to show us that American soldiers did have feelings for Vietnamese people? Is he giving us their perspective? Could he have written this at the time, or only decades later as he reflected on the whole experience?

The conversation shifted again. Were we simply talking about physical distance, or was race creeping in? Could American soldiers ever have looked at the Vietnamese as people? Now Lauren and I had to probe carefully and guide the conversation with our own receptors open. Americans in the United States might have known the Vietnamese only in relation to the war. Lauren had a personal perspective to bring to the table—she had made a visit to the War Atrocities Museum in Saigon / Ho Chi Minh City. She recalled how the museum quickly gave another perspective of the war, but one that was schizophrenic, with its American tanks, planes, and guns seemingly displayed triumphantly in the courtyard, its deformed babies in jars, and its room full of war protest memorabilia from around the world. Many of our students had been to Vietnam on a cultural, service, or vacation trip. Had they ever had a conversation with Vietnamese individuals? The kids who had gone on service trips clearly had—to them, it wasn't that much of a stretch to imagine getting to know someone from Vietnam. Yes, there was a language barrier, but they had learned to talk with people with their hands, gestures, and smiles. They felt a genuine attachment to the Vietnamese babies they had held and played with in orphanages; they thought about what those babies' futures might be. Most of the students, however, knew the Vietnamese only as waiters, desk clerks, and nameless characters on the streets, some with scary deformities, others following them to beg for money. Perhaps most important to our discussion, though, was the fact that unlike Americans in the United States, few thought of the Vietnamese as the enemy.

What emerged was fascinating as the students stepped outside of their intellectual roles, their classroom, and their book-learned and movie-influenced selves and tried to place themselves in Vietnam again—now with gun in hand. It is amazing how easy it is for teachers and students to let all historical study be intensely abstract, completely removed from their own deepening understanding of the complexities of human interactions. To them, historical figures were never real people—they had all been reduced to boxed, fully interpreted bits of information. But all it takes is reminding students that they do know something about how people act, and then ask them to draw on their personal experiences to get them to entertain the possibility that an American soldier like O'Brien could come to know something deep and personal about his enemy. For a brief moment in class many of our students truly felt what O'Brien was trying to convey—that soldiers can agonize over pulling the trigger, can imagine their enemy as people, and can feel remorse at their actions in battle even when they are "only doing their jobs."

But as anyone who knows the book well might predict, for students this moment of realization was clouded by a growing concern with the veracity of the narrative. Tim, whose voice invariably carried authority in class, spoke up. "But wait a minute, how does O'Brien know this about the man he killed? Even if he did go back later and find all this stuff out, the story is told as if O'Brien knows this as he sits on the ground staring at the dead soldier."

Liz, our inveterate literature buff, tried to defend O'Brien's story. "No, he doesn't say he knows the guy's background; he infers it at that moment based on what the guy is carrying, the ring on his finger, his physique, and the ease with which O'Brien was able to kill him."

"So why write the story as if the part about just arriving home from school is true? Are we to believe that O'Brien acted on his intuition and interviewed family members later on?"

"Of course not—the point is that O'Brien walks right up to the guy and stares—looks deeply at the man he killed, emblazons the vision on his mind so that he can never forget the wrenching details."

A bit lost, Aaron interjected at this point, "But, uh, Mr. James, Ms. Jackson—is this story true?"

Students recalled that in an earlier story O'Brien had told us that he had made up all the details of Curt Lemon's death so that we would understand that true war stories aren't about war. They are about sunlight, about "how you must cross the river and march into the mountains and do things you are afraid to do. [They're] about love and memory" (85). Clearly we were getting somewhere. We now seemed collectively to have taken one step closer to understanding what O'Brien meant by "story truth." We had just had a conversation about how soldiers can really feel remorse about what they do in battle— that they can empathize with the enemy. The students could no longer believe that soldiers do what they have to do and it was all simply acceptable.

But in ours, and O'Brien's, moment of glory, when the light was shining most clearly on the concept of story truth, we also realized that the Vietnamese once again drop out of the story. O'Brien can't have it both ways. His story about the man he killed isn't about the man he killed at all. All that is entirely made up, and O'Brien can't pretend to have ever gotten inside the heads of the Vietnamese. The story is about O'Brien, period. It of course felt good to take a step closer to understanding the power and importance of story truth for historical and literary inquiry.

There was also a twinge of anxiety for us as teachers—we couldn't pretend that we were exposing our students to multiple perspectives on the Vietnam War by having them read *The Things They Carried*. To expose anyone to truly diverse perspectives, we had to get them to read more than one great book. (Bao Ninh's *Sorrow of War: A Novel of North Vietnam* is a marvelous, and equally personal, companion in this regard.)

But ultimately, *The Things They Carried* is a phenomenal tool for reinforcing the concept of multiple perspectives. O'Brien is quite self-conscious about his viewpoint; he's always pointing it out to us, interjecting his present self into the book, reminding us that he's not a soldier anymore but a middle-aged writer (with a questioning daughter) who has studied and revisited Vietnam. At the same time, he insists that it's not all relative. His perspective *is* truth. He is telling us these stories to "help to clarify and explain." Knowing that multiple perspectives exist and learning about them is not a license to be indifferent, to throw up our hands and say, "How can we really know the truth about anything?" We hoped that our students had understood that we must pull the perspectives together to reach a complex and informed conclusion. Most important, we hoped they had learned to reserve judgment of others until they knew the other's story truth.

• TRUE WAR STORIES •

See also "Fictional War Stories" in the subject index.

• PARALLEL UNIVERSES OF HUMAN EXPERIENCE •

• THE *RASHOMON* EFFECT: FICTION AND NONFICTION TOLD FROM SHIFTING PERSPECTIVES •

How it matters where you stand.

RECOMMENDED GREAT BOOKS FOR HIGH SCHOOL KIDS

Ackerman, Diane
A NATURAL HISTORY OF THE SENSES
Diane Ackerman does a delightful job of mixing personal reflection, scientific and anthropological information, and wonderful
writing to visit all five of our senses. Great stuff for poets. My
students' favorite little piece is "The Kiss," in the chapter titled
"Touch."

Adisa, Opal Palmer
IT BEGINS WITH TEARS
From the first page of this book, you are thrown into a wild,
raunchy, and intensely loving village in Jamaica. Adisa gives us
new insights into the complexities of a community's web, as well
as into women's secrets.

Aeschylus
THE ORESTEIA
See page 61.

Agee, James
A DEATH IN THE FAMILY
This delicately and perceptively written book explores the impact
of a father's sudden and accidental death on a small family. Oddly,

when I read it in high school, I thought it exposed the tawdriness of this family. Rereading it as an adult, I felt much more empathy for the family. Different views at different ages.

Albee, Edward
WHO'S AFRAID OF VIRGINIA WOOLF?
This painful confrontation between a smart and destructive man and woman was written in 1962, and no one has been able to, or even tried to, top this play's brutal word duel in a failed relationship.

Alexie, Sherman
THE LONE RANGER AND TONTO FISTFIGHT IN HEAVEN
Revisit Thomas, Victor, Junior, and a slew of other characters in this beautiful, funny, and devastating collection of short stories offering glimpses into modern life on the Indian reservation. Alexie is one of the great, funny, deep, and affecting young Native American writers of today. The fine film *Smoke Signals* was based on this book.

Alexie, Sherman
RESERVATION BLUES
See page 91.

Alexie, Sherman
TEN LITTLE INDIANS
Alexie's latest book is arguably his best. Savor his language, his humor, his characters, and his storytelling flair in stories about a forty-year-old wannabe basketball star and an Indian poet who "faked" it.

Alexie, Sherman
THE TOUGHEST INDIAN IN THE WORLD
Another collection of short stories by Alexie, this one doesn't shy away from sex, which appears in many forms. Funny, sad, and deeply disturbing, these stories show Alexie taking some risks with content and style, and the risks pay off.

Allison, Dorothy
BASTARD OUT OF CAROLINA
See page 1.

Allison, Dorothy
TWO OR THREE THINGS I KNOW FOR SURE
Check out the real family of Allison in this autobiographical and photographic look at her life.

Alter, Peter
GENESIS
Translated as modern poetry, this book offers a new look at the foundational story of Western thought. Somehow the new language can break you out of the ritualistic gauze that the old translations put over the stories, and it makes you wonder about the ideas, concerns, and tribal imperatives that drove the story.

Alvarez, Julia
HOW THE GARCIA GIRLS LOST THEIR ACCENTS
This story, which traces a Dominican family of girls living in the United States back to their roots, is funny, poignant, and told backwards. Explore the Dominican culture, both in its native land and in this transplanted family. See also her family portrait, *Yo!*

Alvarez, Julia
IN THE TIME OF THE BUTTERFLIES
A gripping political and personal tale of resistance to Rafael Trujillo's dictatorship in the Dominican Republic of the 1950s, this is the true story of three sisters who gave their lives up in the struggle, and the fourth one who lived to tell about it.

Anaya, Rudolfo
BLESS ME, ULTIMA
See page 78.

Anderson, Laurie Halse
SPEAK
Melinda was emotionally and socially paralyzed by an event at a party the summer before high school started, and she can't heal until she finds her voice again. In a series of journal entries, report cards, and even messages from the school's bathroom walls, the author conveys a vivid message of both warning and empowerment for young women.

Anderson, Sherwood
WINESBURG, OHIO
This outstanding collection of interrelated short stories is set in turn-of-the-century (no, not 2000, 1900!) rural Ohio. Anderson's dark psychological explorations are unmatched. A must-read for any fan of Salinger.

Ansary, Tamim
WEST OF KABUL, EAST OF NEW YORK
This book is one of the most compelling memoirs of our time. Ansary grew up in Afghanistan until he reached the age of sixteen, after which he moved to the United States. He has fine insight into the world of Islam as well as into the Western way of thinking. His tale is a great cross-cultural journey, so important in today's epic confrontation between the United States and the Islamic world. *West of Kabul* will take you miles ahead of most U.S. policymakers in understanding Afghan culture.

Apollo
CONCRETE CANDY
This gripping collection of short stories is written by a teenager and deals with the struggle to survive in today's cities. Apollo's stories present a truthful portrayal of youths in the streets of Oakland, California.

Armstrong, Karen
THE BATTLE FOR GOD
This is an insightful exploration of the rise of fundamentalism in the modern world. Armstrong takes a look at recent radical turns

in Islam, Christianity, and Judaism. This topic is even more compelling since 9/11. Armstrong, a former nun, is also the author of
The History of God and *Islam: A Short History.*

Atwood, Margaret
THE BLIND ASSASSIN
Jon Carroll, my favorite *San Francisco Chronicle* columnist, gives
this one highest praise: "It's a perfect summer book—it contains
suicide, betrayal, hot cheap sex, wicked sisters, and very large
boats—and it is written in a way that makes other writers immediately decide to take night-school courses in locksmithing."

Atwood, Margaret
THE HANDMAID'S TALE
This novel was included in the American Library Association's list
of books that were most commonly banned and censored.
An exaggerated yet hauntingly truthful tale of censorship and
oppression, *The Handmaid's Tale* takes place in a future where
women are no longer allowed to read, let alone think or function
independently.

Bahrampour, Tara
TO SEE AND SEE AGAIN
Learn about three generations of history and culture while reading the gripping memoir of a young girl with an Iranian father
and a Californian mother. Together, they travel back and forth between Iran and the United States during the Iranian Revolution.

Baldwin, James
ANOTHER COUNTRY
Immersed in love, lust, and music in the New York of the early
1960s, the characters in this book cross racial boundaries in a time
when this was taboo. Baldwin continues to be a favorite for
thoughtful young readers. An early gay novel is *Giovanni's Room,*
and for a look at life in the black church, check out his *Go Tell It
on the Mountain.*

Baldwin, James
THE FIRE NEXT TIME
Baldwin's understanding of and insights into race and the American dilemma hold up stronger than almost anything from the 1960s. This series of essays, along with *Notes of a Native Son*, still deliver the most powerful indictment of racism in the United States.

Ballard, Allen
WHERE I'M BOUND
A leading teacher of African American studies at State University of New York, Ballard details the long-overlooked role of a black cavalry regiment that fought for the Union in Mississippi in the last two years of the Civil War. This story makes the film *Glory* look like an insignificant aside.

Bambara, Toni Cade
GORILLA, MY LOVE
This book made some of us laugh until tears ran down our faces. At the same time this tale is smart, critical, and powerfully African American. Told in fifteen short stories that take place in New York and North Carolina, Bambara's book will introduce you to unforgettable characters.

Banks, Russell
CLOUDSPLITTER
One of the truly great historical novels, this book tells the story of the family of John Brown, the white abolitionists who fought a guerrilla war in Kansas against the slavers trying to take over the state and then attacked Harper's Ferry in Virginia in an attempt to launch a slave revolt. You will truly feel the characters' world and understand their daring and their radical clarity. A brilliant, insightful meditation on American culture and history.

Banks, Russell
CONTINENTAL DRIFT
This heartbreaking story of longing follows the collision course of two families from opposite sides of the world—a beautifully written tale of heroic characters in the tragic pursuit of happiness.

Banks, Russell
RULE OF THE BONE
Whether a hero's journey, an antihero's journey, or a spiritual journey, this modern *Catcher in the Rye* is poignant and riveting. I've yet to meet a teenager who doesn't fall under the spell of Bone, a troubled and insightful young teen. Follow him from upstate New York to Jamaica in his quest for truth and meaning.

Barker, Pat
REGENERATION
The Brits have a bunch of amazing novelists, and Barker is the leader of the pack. This World War I tale is stunning. Imagine the moral dilemmas of a shrink whose job is to cure patients driven insane by the madness of war—so they can return to the front! The first (and best) of a trilogy.

Bates, Karen Grigsby
PLAIN BROWN WRAPPER
Follow the adventures of L.A. newspaper columnist Alex Powell— adventure, murder mystery, and a look at African American journalism.

Berry, Wendell
LIFE IS A MIRACLE: AN ESSAY
AGAINST MODERN SUPERSTITION
Anything written by this author can give kids new ideas about our world. An environmentalist, essayist, and farmer, Berry is a poet and a visionary. Sometimes a true understanding of our ecosystems is more awe inspiring than vague religious exhortations. Check out some of his other books, such as *The Unsettling of America: Culture and Agriculture, What Are People For?* and *Sex, Economy, Freedom, and Community.*

Bloch, Ariel and Chana
THE SONG OF SONGS
This new translation of the Song of Songs, or Song of Solomon, from the Hebrew Bible restores the book to the erotic, passionate love poem that it is. If you have read Toni Morrison's novel, you'll want to revisit the biblical book it is named after.

Block, Francesca Lia
WEETZIE BAT
Block's series, which begins with this novella, is fun, fast, affecting, and very L.A. Bookstore managers typically don't know where to put this book: young adult? (too sexy), normal fiction? (too young). Just read it.

Boyle, T. C.
TORTILLA CURTAIN
In this smart, easy read, Boyle explores the conflicts and contradictions of the border—the parallel lives of Mexican immigrant and yuppie couples. Boyle captures the minutiae of everyday hypocrisies.

Bradbury, Ray
FAHRENHEIT 451
A fireman whose job is burning books struggles to understand how censorship affects society. If you haven't read it yet, you should.

Brontë, Charlotte
JANE EYRE
A classic and compelling story of obsessive love set in nineteenth-century England, this book is a Victorian thriller that young readers can't put down. (Follow it up with Jean Rhys's *Wide Sargasso Sea* for a feminist rewrite from the perspective of the mysterious first wife of Rochester.)

Brontë, Emily
WUTHERING HEIGHTS
Get swept up in the gothic drama of the infamous love story of Cathy and Heathcliff! Haunting and intense, this classic is a passionate tale of revenge and romance.

Burciaga, José Antonio
DRINK CULTURA: CHICANISMO
More than a history of the southwestern and western Chicano experience, *Drink Cultura* is a wild ride through Burciaga's mind and heart, sort of a Chicano *On the Road* (see Jack Kerouac).

Burgess, Anthony
A CLOCKWORK ORANGE
Burgess has given us a frightening glimpse at a near-future world marked by roving gangs of youth who seek entertainment in "ultra-violence" and a society that experiments with drastic measures to control the impending anarchy.

Burroughs, William
NAKED LUNCH
This quasi-hallucinogenic novel will gross you out, make you wonder, and challenge your ideas. Burroughs's exploration of the dregs of our society and our subconscious—as he throws himself into prison, an addiction to heroin, and worse—developed a cult following in the 1960s and has recently been revived.

Butler, Octavia
PARABLE OF THE TALENTS
Butler is one of the deepest-thinking African American authors, combining a huge imagination with deep social insights. This is the second in the Earthseed series and offers a futuristic nightmare of a collapsing society—and young visionaries who try to forge a new understanding for survival. Her *Kindred* is another favorite.

Camus, Albert
THE STRANGER
This is a must-read if you want to pretend you're in a café in Paris, hunched over your yellow journal with a Gaulois hanging out of your mouth, contemplating whether we are anything but ephemeral dust. I don't really mean to make fun of it, though, as Camus was a radical critic of European self-satisfaction after World War II.

Canada, Geoffrey
FIST STICK KNIFE GUN
A memoir of coming of age in South Bronx, Canada's book has become a must-read for many teens. The escalation of weapons in youth violence is a terrifying development that the adult world has brought about.

Carroll, Jim
THE BASKETBALL DIARIES
This is a gritty coming-of-age story about the poet Jim Carroll, a New York teen addicted to drugs and searching for something pure. It's dark and difficult and makes you cringe, but it's well written and real.

Castellanos, Rosario
THE NINE GUARDIANS
This beautiful book about the Mexican Revolution was written by a woman who went on to found the Ballet Folklorico of Mexico. The novel tells of the revolution's impact on the rural area of Chiapas at a time when the Indian people threw off their landlords. Castellanos combines a deep understanding of the Mayan people's struggles with a keen insight into how the oppression of women fits in Mexican class society.

Castillo, Ana
SO FAR FROM GOD
This book contains wonderful stories of New Mexico's Chicano life from a woman's point of view. It depicts a mother and four daughters you won't forget.

Chabon, Michael
THE AMAZING ADVENTURES
OF KAVALIER & CLAY

This novel reveals the real genesis of American comic books. The Jewish immigrants on the margins of society who brought us vaudeville and delicatessens also created this slice of pop culture. Chabon weaves the history of the Golem, the Holocaust, Superman, and the transitions to post–World War II suburbia in a story of start-up comics and epic struggles with evil characters you will never forget. I hate blurbs that read "rollicking tale," but this one demands it. See also his *Wonder Boys* and *Mysteries of Pittsburgh*.

Chbosky, Stephen
THE PERKS OF BEING A WALLFLOWER

Told from the viewpoint of an immensely likable fourteen-year-old, *Perks* is the story of an intelligent and funny boy figuring out the complexities of his life. Often regarded as a contemporary of *Catcher in the Rye* (see J. D. Salinger), this book is perhaps more raw and even funnier, and it certainly offers more connections to most teenagers than the prep-school life of Holden Caulfield.

Chevalier, Tracy
GIRL WITH A PEARL EARRING

This book is the coming-of-age story of sixteen-year-old Griet in the Holland of the 1660s. A tale of awakening and art, it takes a famous Vermeer painting by the same title as an imaginative starting point. A historical novel that will make real the way that sixteen-year-olds today have a lot in common with sixteen-year-olds four hundred years ago.

Chin, Frank
DONALD DUK

This book is a lovely story of a twelve-year-old second-generation immigrant in San Francisco's Chinatown.

Chopin, Kate
THE AWAKENING
This turn-of-the-century story of a modern woman seeking fulfillment in a prohibitive time and place is riveting, illuminating, frustrating, and devastating. It may help today's women to understand how far we've come.

Cisneros, Sandra
HOUSE ON MANGO STREET
Well, many of you read this novel in high school or even middle school. If you didn't, run out and buy it. A series of autobiographical vignettes, *Mango Street* is one of the great short identity prose-poems. You will also likely enjoy Cisneros's hilarious and open-hearted poetry in her book *My Wicked, Wicked Ways*.

Coelho, Paulo
THE ALCHEMIST
Learn about world cultures and religions while being captivated by a spiritual journey that traverses southern Europe and northern Africa. Teens relate to Santiago's pursuit of a dream, which ultimately becomes a quest for self-knowledge and acceptance.

Colton, Larry
COUNTING COUP: A TRUE STORY OF BASKETBALL AND HONOR ON THE LITTLE BIG HORN
You have probably seen the movie *Hoop Dreams*—about the basketball ambitions of Chicago teenagers—or even read the book (see Ben Joravsky). Well, this is a different take on the city game. A teenage Lakota Sioux Indian girl and her team fight their way to respect and awareness in their pursuit of the high school state title. A great read. A similar tale is told for Navajo girls' basketball in the film *Rocks with Wings*.

Connell, Evan
DEUS LO VOLT: CHRONICLE OF THE CRUSADES
This rather strange novel is written in a hand that purports to be from the time of the Crusades, like a running journal. It gets kids

to think about this strange chapter in Western history. What drove Europeans to send huge armies to the East? What legacies from this sordid period (such as colonialism, the Middle East conflict, and so on) do we still grapple with?

Crane, Stephen
THE RED BADGE OF COURAGE
In this classic nineteenth-century Civil War story, Stephen Crane launches an attack on the grim realities of war from an individual soldier's perspective. Crane enters the mind of a soldier who is obsessed with his fears and how he performs in battle in the presence of his comrades. This book is often assigned in class, but don't let that ruin it for you. Crane writes with an honesty and ethic that say he is trying to save your life.

Dana, Richard Henry
TWO YEARS BEFORE THE MAST
Imagine a nineteenth-century Harvard graduate who decides to sign on as a sailor on a ship going from New England to California and back (around the bottom of South America). This book's language may be slightly old-fashioned, but it is still a wild ride. Think nineteenth-century extreme sports.

Danticat, Edwidge
BREATH, EYES, MEMORY
This book is the beautiful story of a Haitian girl named Sophie who is moved from her rural island life to New York. Danticat has such an ear for dialogue and an eye for the telling detail that you will read it like poetry.

Diamant, Anita
THE RED TENT
This modern novel is about the biblical tale of Dinah, daughter of Jacob, retold from the point of view of a female writer. Dinah is in the women's tent, where birthing, menses, and illnesses are confined and where she shares the stories of her four mothers

(Jacob's four wives), as well as of her own struggles. It makes you think about what the Bible doesn't show us about ancient history and the founding stories of Western civilization.

Diamond, Jared
GUNS, GERMS, AND STEEL
Lots of college freshmen are assigned this book, and high school kids can handle it too. It will expand your thinking on how and why events happen in history. The idea for the book came when Diamond was asked by Yali, a local man in New Guinea, "Why is it that the white people have developed so much cargo?" The answer became a lifelong quest to understand wealth, poverty, and history.

Dick, Philip
MAN IN THE HIGH CASTLE
Written in the 1950s, this novel presupposes that the Japanese and Germans have won World War II. Japanese tourists snap up "authentic American" chachkis in San Francisco, and German diplomats fly across the Atlantic on Von Braun rockets. Dick is one of the most passionately read fantasy/sci-fi novelists. His other books include *Do Androids Dream of Electric Sheep?* (on which *Blade Runner* is based), *A Scanner Darkly*, and *The Simulacra*.

Di Prima, Diane
RECOLLECTIONS OF MY LIFE AS A WOMAN: THE NEW YORK YEARS
This is a fascinating memoir by one of the great writers of the Beatnik era (see Jack Kerouac) and early feminists—a long book but not at all a "difficult" read. Lots of delightful stories. Maybe your mom will remember her Beatnik days and buy it for you.

Dorris, Michael
A YELLOW RAFT IN BLUE WATER
Secrets and a generation gap threaten to break apart a Native American family, but Dorris braids together three generations of women by letting each one tell her own version of the story. Accessible, gripping, and poignant, this is Dorris's best novel and is often read in schools.

Dostoyevsky, Fyodor
CRIME AND PUNISHMENT
This book is a must. Russian novels are often lurching, obsessive journeys through insane landscapes. And here Dostoyevsky presents one of the great madmen of literature, Raskolnikov, a starving student who tells the tale of why he felt compelled to kill his landlady. Hint: it had something to do with mastering the powers of life and death. This book is long but very much worth the effort.

Doyle, Roddy
PADDY CLARKE HA HA HA
In this book, ten-year-old Irish boys get into mischief and wonder about life. Told flawlessly from the viewpoint of a child, this novel is about growth and the confusion that accompanies it.

Dry, Richard
LEAVING
Dry follows four generations of an African American family in Oakland, California (and from the South). This portrait takes us from the early migrations to the shipyard jobs of World War II, to the birth of the Black Panthers, and up to the devastations caused by the crack epidemic.

Dunn, Katherine
GEEK LOVE
This is a bizarre tale of a circus family who dabble in a sort of perverted eugenics in order to create a family of sideshow freaks.

Eggers, Dave
A HEARTBREAKING WORK OF
STAGGERING GENIUS
In this mostly autobiographical work, college-age Dave suddenly finds himself the guardian of his seven-year-old brother and faces various dilemmas such as choosing between going clubbing and attending a PTA meeting. This book is both wrenching and hilarious. Eggers has become a creative writing phenomenon, run-

ning extensive workshops for teens, spearheading the creation of *McSweeney's,* a literary magazine, and most recently publishing the youth hit novel *You Shall Know Our Velocity!*

Ehrenreich, Barbara
NICKEL AND DIMED
Journalist Ehrenreich relates her jobs as a waitress, maid, and retailer in Florida, Maine, and Minnesota in an effort to find out how people on minimum wage survive. Learn about economics in an interesting way.

Elliot, Stephen
A LIFE WITHOUT CONSEQUENCES
Stephen Elliot describes the life of a teenage runaway in Chicago—a modern-day Dante's *Inferno.* This look at the underbelly of the American bubble reminds us of the beauty of the human spirit and the many paths to redemption.

Ellison, Ralph
INVISIBLE MAN
No, this is not the science fiction book on which the movie is based. Rather, it is a classic black novel that has been attacked by everyone from the Left to the Right. The odyssey of a nameless narrator, it is a journey from the South to New York's Harlem and also through the whole labyrinth of American race politics and insanity. Since it has been categorized as a "black book," most people have not noticed that *Invisible Man* is also a leading example of existential, modern fiction. You should read this one about once a year.

Erdrich, Louise
TRACKS
Louise Erdrich tells a whole series of amazing first-person stories, giving a realistic version of Native American life that is quite different from the stories of idealized or demonized Indians found in much of U.S. literature. Many of her books are fantastic,

including *The Beet Queen, Love Medicine, The Master Butchers Singing Club,* and even the children's book *The Birchbark House.*

Escandón, María Amparo
ESPERANZA'S BOX OF SAINTS
This is a small book that has had a big impact on a number of students. Esperanza is a woman from a small town in Mexico whose daughter went in for surgery and was reported to have died. Convinced that her daughter has in fact been sold into prostitution, Esperanza travels from bordello to bordello, all the way up to Los Angeles, seeking the truth.

Esquivel, Laura
LIKE WATER FOR CHOCOLATE
A delightful introduction to Latin American magical realism, Esquivel's novel draws you in and takes you on a wild ride of passion repressed and expressed. This is also a women's book, one that uncovers the hidden traditions passed on in kitchens and cookbooks, as well as bedroom secrets. Once I went to a *Like Water for Chocolate* party where each person had to bring a dish from one of the chapters!

Fadiman, Ann
THE SPIRIT CATCHES YOU AND YOU FALL DOWN
Epilepsy among the Hmong is seen as a gift, just as schizophrenics are revered as shamans in many cultures. Here the tragic misunderstandings between cultures are amazing. This book will change the way you think about the experiences of people who are new to America.

Faulks, Sebastian
BIRDSONG
This is a strange novel that jumps around to three moments in time but has one of the most powerful evocations of trench warfare (in World War I) ever written.

Fitch, Janet
WHITE OLEANDER
A mother and a daughter share secrets and struggles. Astrid, the teenager, is forced to invent a new identity when her mother goes to prison for poisoning her boyfriend. This is another one of those books that are passed from hand to hand—especially by teenage girls.

Fitzgerald, F. Scott
THE GREAT GATSBY
In the off chance that you are in one of the few high schools that don't read this in American Lit., it's worth your while. Packed with fated love, shady business, and lovely language, it's a fun read that conveys the flavor of the Roaring Twenties.

Fleming, Keith
THE BOY WITH A THORN
IN HIS SIDE: A MEMOIR
This book is a memoir of a teen's troubles and the loving uncle who helped him understand himself and work his way through deep alienation. The uncle is the gay author Edmund White, whose fictional version of the same story is the 1997 novel *The Farewell Symphony*. The memoir offers a surprising and new look at how families, love, and transformation work.

Fox, Paula
BORROWED FINERY
This book is an amazing memoir that follows the story of a strong girl from her abandonment in New York, to life in Cuba, and to the seedy side of Hollywood.

Franken, Al
LIES AND THE LYING LIARS WHO TELL THEM
Al Franken takes on the conservative media with this personal brand of satire and wit. A comical dissection of right-wing punditry.

Frazier, Charles
COLD MOUNTAIN
Cold Mountain is a gorgeously descriptive love story set during the Civil War. You are drawn slowly but inexorably into the life of an injured southern war deserter and of the woman he is walking south to see again. Frazier provides a plausible and thought-provoking tale of how the Civil War affected southern civilians as the war came to a close.

French, Albert
BILLY
This novel is a terrifyingly accurate portrayal of Mississippi in the 1930s in which a fight with white kids leads to the execution of a black minor.

Fumia, Molly
HONOR THY CHILDREN
In this moving memoir, a Japanese American family learns difficult lessons from a son who has AIDS.

Gaarder, Jostein
SOPHIE'S WORLD
Sophie's World is a fictional story that also relates the history of philosophy. It is easy to read and informative, even if a bit Western and strong on Christianity.

Gaiman, Neil
AMERICAN GODS
All the ancient gods from around the world have migrated to America along with their believers, but belief is dying out as they are being replaced by new, more technological deities. Who will win? This book is a mind-bender (plus it is fun to try to figure out which mythical character is who).

Gaines, Ernest J.
A GATHERING OF OLD MEN
This is an excellent book about racial tension written from shifting perspectives. Hear the story behind the death of a Cajun farmer from each member of a group of black men.

Gaines, Ernest J.
A LESSON BEFORE DYING
This book is the heart-wrenching story of a condemned man learning to read from a young teacher. It contains powerful reflections on education, racism, punishment, and the meaning of our humanity.

Galeano, Eduardo
OPEN VEINS OF LATIN AMERICA
Galeano is a Che Guevara with a poetry journal. His biting analysis is mixed with soaring prose. You haven't understood the Americas if you haven't read this guy. Galeano has also written a fine book on soccer *(Soccer in Sun and Shadow)* and a trilogy called *Memory of Fire*, a history of Latin America—all told in short anecdotes rendered in his utterly poetic hand.

Gardner, John
GRENDEL
Grendel is the story of Beowulf written from the monster's point of view. If you think *your* parents are odd, wait until you meet his mom!

Garland, Alex
THE BEACH
A modern-day *Lord of the Flies* set in tropical Thailand, this gripping adventure story depicts a Utopian retreat gone bad. You won't be able to put the book down. Don't judge a book by the movie!

Gates, Jr., Henry Louis
THE BONDWOMAN'S NARRATIVE,
BY HANNAH CRAFTS
Gates bought an old manuscript at an auction and discovered that he had acquired a unique and critical piece of history—a narrative by a slave who furtively obtained a powerful literary education. The book is a great read. Gates's excitement, expressed in the introduction, is also worth the price of the book.

Ghosh, Amitav
THE GLASS PALACE
This work is a tremendous historical sweep extending from the British colonial conquest of Burma and India through World Wars I and II, all the way through the 1990s. I can't get the story of Rajkumar, Dolly, and the others out of my head. The book is an incredible exposé of imperialism as well as a powerful personal story.

Gogol, Nicolai
DEAD SOULS
According to Nabokov, *Dead Souls* is the best Russian novel ever written, and it really is a riotous class satire. Sometimes you just don't want to pick up one more book about teenage angst, risk-taking, and self-absorption will find that Gogol is the remedy. This author will transport them to the Russian tundras of the nineteenth century, where they will meet a man who buys up the paperwork of dead peasants so he can use it as a tax break. In this morbidly hilarious book, Gogol creates unforgettable characters.

Goines, Donald
DADDY COOL AND DOPE FIEND
One of the most popular African American authors, Goines, along with Iceberg Slim, kept the bus-stop paperback publisher Holloway House in business with hard-edged, vernacular-laced, and in-your-face 1960s tales.

Goldberg, Myla
BEE SEASON

Bee Season is a beautifully written first novel that follows a family's deterioration as each member pursues a secret passion toward estrangement. Although it begins as a funny story, later it turns serious. It is both riveting and disturbing.

Gordon, Neil
THE COMPANY YOU KEEP

This book is about young radicals going underground to fight the U.S. government in the 1960s and middle-aged fugitives still working out their complex paths. This is a story takes you into a world of revolutionary idealism, romance, and fear—all through a series of e-mails that carry the story. The theme of parents and their kids runs throughout the novel.

Gould, Stephen Jay
THE HEDGEHOG, THE FOX, AND THE MAGISTER'S POX: MENDING THE GAP BETWEEN SCIENCE AND THE HUMANITIES

Read anything by this guy, the great evolutionary biologist and ethicist. Gould died in 2002 and has left a hole in the world of popular science writing. If you really want to "get it" about evolution and how we came to be here, read this accessible and wonderful book. Gould decided to become a paleontologist after a childhood visit to the New York Museum of Natural History. Gould is evolution's most eloquent defender and explainer, even if he criticizes people who think they can explain all human behavior by appealing to simple evolutionary stories.

Gourevitch, Philip
WE WISH TO INFORM YOU THAT TOMORROW WE WILL BE KILLED WITH OUR FAMILIES: STORIES FROM RWANDA
Gourevitch provides an insight into the 1994 Rwanda genocide and its roots in European colonialism. This book is extremely painful to read, but it will give you a perspective on recent world events that you won't see on the evening news.

Grass, Günter
THE TIN DRUM
This book is the challenging, bittersweet, but often hilarious story of a small boy who literally refuses to grow up.

Guest, Judith
ORDINARY PEOPLE
This heart-wrenching novel about a family in crisis resonates with all readers. A teenage boy's suicide attempt results in a stay in a mental institution, but it is the family dynamics—particularly his mother's reaction—that make this book so realistic and powerful.

Guterson, David
EAST OF THE MOUNTAINS
This is a beautiful and lyrical tale of the journey of an elderly doctor facing imminent death and figuring out the meaning of life. It may sound dull to the young reader, but believe me, you will love it. Guterson also wrote *Snow Falling on Cedars*, which makes you want to fall in love and make something ethical of your life at the same time.

Hagedorn, Jessica
DOGEATERS
Evoking the shimmering, frightening, and delightful world of a group of teens in Manila during the Marcos period, Hagedorn has created a wild riff on coming-of age-stories. A Filipino version of Gabriel García Márquez's books of magical realism. Check out her newest novel, *Dream Jungle*.

Halaby, Laila
WEST OF THE JORDAN
The lives of four young women, adolescent cousins in the West Bank and Jordan, are woven together in a beautiful portrait of Palestinian life today.

Haley, Alex
THE AUTOBIOGRAPHY OF MALCOLM X
Students love the descriptions of 1940s Harlem and are amazed by the political transformation that made Malcolm X one of the most powerful figures of the twentieth century. This book was written with Alex Haley, author of *Roots*.

Hall, Brian
THE SASKIAD
This is a great story of a thirteen-year-old girl growing up. Yes, there are plenty of "coming of age" books, but this one is for you if you feel alone, misunderstood, and like intellectual geeks. The protagonist goes on an odyssey with her new friend Jane Singh and her seldom-present dad, discovers herself, and finally outgrows her parents' hippy hypocrisies.

Hamper, Ben
RIVETHEAD: TALES FROM THE ASSEMBLY LINE
This series of essays and memoir pieces tells the real-life story of a GM autoworker who is smart enough to see that working on the line could wreck him. He finds ways to subvert the system, from "double-teaming" to writing. The author is featured in Michael Moore's documentary *Roger and Me*—he's the man who goes crazy while driving in his truck to the tune of "Wouldn't It Be Nice," by the Beach Boys. Funny and wrenching at the same time, this is a great read.

Hatch, John
MISSISSIPPI SWAMP
This book is the first of a four-novel series on African Americans who fled the white-dominated South after the Civil War.

Heaney, Seamus
THE CURE AT TROY: A VERSION OF SOPHOCLES' PHILOCTETES

The Greeks get it right again. Philoctetes is angry because he's been slighted. He needs to let go of his whining about his sore foot and help the Greeks at Troy. This translation by the Irish Nobel Prize–winner Seamus Heaney is great.

Hellenga, Robert
THE SIXTEEN PLEASURES

An American young woman goes to Florence to help with flood relief and gains insights into history and herself. This is a favorite of high school girls, as it combines personal affirmation with a great intellectual mystery and a personal romance.

Heller, Joseph
CATCH-22

One of the premier exposés of the horrors of war—Italy in World War II this time—Heller's novel is also a hilarious satire on everything crazy in the modern bureaucratic world. Yossarian, the hero, is perhaps the only equal of Kesey's McMurphy (see Ken Kesey), an everyman fighting against "the system."

Hemingway, Ernest
FOR WHOM THE BELL TOLLS

This guy used to be the favorite of high school kids, but that was, oh, fifty years ago. And yet this famously macho writer's spare prose can still pack a lot of power. This book has the American Robert Jordan fighting alongside the Spanish republicans during the Spanish Civil war in 1937. It has it all: revolutionary fervor, existential resignation, a hot love interest, and philosophical musings. Give it a try. If you like it, go on to read *To Have and Have Not* and *A Farewell to Arms*, at least. (See also Milton Wolff.)

Herbert, Frank
DUNE
In this book characters ride giant worms and create a guerrilla resistance movement—what more could kids want? This science fiction classic is still one of the best. Hint: don't watch the movie version.

Hernandez, Jaime
THE DEATH OF SPEEDY
Jaime Hernandez does his own graphic novel work and pens others with his brother in the stunning *Love and Rockets* series. Always gritty, smart, and captivating.

Hesse, Hermann
SIDDHARTHA
Siddhartha leaves home to find himself, discovers meditation, power, money, and women, and realizes that none of these is the answer to his fundamental questions. This is a favorite of teenagers who find themselves on a quest.

Hillenbrand, Laura
SEABISCUIT
I didn't care a bit for horses or horse racing until I read this riveting account of one of the most compelling underdog horses in American racing history. From the grueling reality of a jockey's life to the rags-to-riches tale of the owner, Hillenbrand makes reading about racing fascinating for the uninitiated.

Hillerman, Tony
THE WAILING WIND
Hillerman has created a series of delightful books. These Native American cultural journeys are part police method and part mystery. In each one (and there are more than fifteen), Navajo tribal cops Joe Leaphorn and Jim Chee get to the bottom of a crime while teaching or learning more about indigenous ways.

Himes, Chester
YESTERDAY WILL MAKE YOU CRY
Himes was the master, the trickster, and the teacher using the cop/mystery genre featuring two African American detectives in Harlem. His book was the basis for the fine film *Cotton Comes to Harlem.*

Holthe, Tess Uriza
WHEN THE ELEPHANTS DANCE
This novel provides a real-life look at Filipino civilians during the Japanese occupation of the Philippines and the American invasion to take it back. Holthe has combined his insights into folk life, a bit of magical realism, and amazing historical detail.

Hornby, Nick
HIGH FIDELITY
List makers and music aficionados will love this book, which is narrated by a British slacker who owns a record store and is a loser in love (and, some might argue, in life). Redrafted into an American setting, this book was made into a great movie. See also Hornby's *About a Boy.*

Hughes, Langston
THE COLLECTED POEMS OF LANGSTON HUGHES
The prolific Hughes was one of the greatest American poets. This volume includes every poem he published in his lifetime, and several published after his death. It's arranged chronologically, which makes it fun to trace the development of his ideas and form. If you want it all, this is the book for you.

Hughes, Langston
SHORT STORIES
This fantastic collection published in 1996 takes kids from Africa to Harlem nightclubs and beautifully captures certain moments in history. Hughes's dignified characters will make you laugh and cry.

Hughes, Langston
THE WAYS OF WHITE FOLKS

This book is full of great observations on race and American culture. Riffing off of the great W. E. B. DuBois classic *The Souls of Black Folk*, Hughes takes an anthropologist's eye and a satirist's pen to the strange ways in which racism works in America. Hughes was a funny and unrelenting African American voice from the Harlem Renaissance to the 1950s. Get anything he wrote.

Hulme, Keri
THE BONE PEOPLE

Three broken strangers—a Maori man, a mute white child, and a woman of mixed blood—must face their pasts to make a future. This captivating tale, set in New Zealand and structured as a great circle, redefines family.

Hurston, Zora Neale
THEIR EYES WERE WATCHING GOD

This book is an empowering story about a woman with the strength to find independence at a time when this meant bucking society's norms. This lyrical novel, written in dialect, is a must-read for all human beings.

Huxley, Aldous
BRAVE NEW WORLD

Huxley is better than Orwell at imagining a horrid future controlled by the government. Only here, instead of being kept in place by jack-booted troopers, we are controlled by psychological means—mood drugs, biologically engineered personalities, and soft chains of control. Sound even more like today? You will recognize lots of it.

Irving, John
THE WORLD ACCORDING TO GARP

This novel chronicles the unconventional life of the son of a nurse. It deals with feminism, love, marriage, sex, parenthood, writing, tolerance, and integrity. Humorous yet bittersweet, this gripping novel will inspire smiles and tears at the same time. Other books for Irving aficionados are *The Hotel New Hampshire* and *A Prayer for Owen Meany.*

Ives, David
ALL IN THE TIMING
This book is a hilarious and occasionally profane collection of satirical short plays that stretch and twist the English language in original and insightful ways. What do the infamous chimps typing Shakespeare really have to say? What if a restaurant served only the opposite of what customers ordered? Can all of David Mamet's plays be condensed into ten minutes? If you love contemporary plays, this book is for you.

Jackson, Phil
SACRED HOOPS
The Chicago Bulls, Michael Jordan, and Zen Buddhism—what more do we need to say? This book was written by the legendary and meditating powerhouse coach of the Bulls.

Johnson, Charles
MIDDLE PASSAGE
This historical novel about the African slave trade tells of the horrors of a slave ship as seen through the eyes of a free black man. In this compelling read, Johnson has crafted a literary masterpiece.

Jones, LeRoi
BLUES PEOPLE
Learn about the history of black music in America as told by lauded poet and playwright known today as Amiri Baraka.

Jones, Solomon
PIPE DREAM
This is about crack addicts in Philadelphia, an inverse look at who are "good guys" and "bad guys." In form, it's a murder mystery

about wrongly accused addicts on the run. We learn their sad back stories and identify with them fully. This book was written by a Philadelphian journalist-novelist.

Joravsky, Ben
HOOP DREAMS

You may have seen the great documentary of the Chicago high school ball and dreams of the NBA. This book goes deeper. The desperate, and usually impossible, dream of making it in professional sports is exposed with heartbreaking truthfulness.

Karr, Mary
LIARS' CLUB

Karr's matter-of-fact reporting of life from the point of view of a seven-year-old with a crazy mom is a real grabber. Her next novel, *Cherry*, takes it up to the girl's teen years, and is a much deeper and more insightful memoir than most of the books on the shelves these days.

Katz, Jonathan
GEEKS: HOW TWO LOST BOYS RODE THE INTERNET OUT OF IDAHO

This fascinating story about computer nerds who almost slipped through the cracks is a page-turner that reveals something about escaping the limited mindset of the community in which we grew up.

Katzenberger, Elaine, ed.
FIRST WORLD, HA HA HA: THE ZAPATISTA CHALLENGE

This collection of articles provides insight into the Chiapas rebellion in Mexico. If you want your kids to understand our modern world, the impact of globalism, and NAFTA, have them check this one out. You may end up joining the many young people protesting world trade practices. Here's some political insight you won't find in your local newspaper.

Kawabata, Yasunari
SNOW COUNTRY
Incredibly, this Nobel Prize–winning author captures the honesty and tragic trust of a Japanese country geisha named Komako. This book will transport you to the unforgettable world of a young woman.

Kay, Guy Gavriel
TIGANA
In a world of magic and gritty reality, a group of resisters seeks to break the grip of a tyrant. One of the coolest fantasy books, *Tigana* is terrifying and exhilarating at the same time.

Kaysen, Susanna
GIRL, INTERRUPTED
This account of Kaysen's stay in a mental institution as a young woman is a quick and interesting read that challenges our notions about mental illness and being female in our society.

Keegan, John
THE FACE OF BATTLE
This is an original look at the realities of war for the common guy on the ground, highlighting three epochal battles in history: in 1415, 1815, and 1916. Keegan has done his historical research and focuses on real, horrific battlegrounds instead of generals' tents, which most war stories depict.

Kerouac, Jack
ON THE ROAD
In this classic 1950s road book, a group of alienated men traipse back and forth across the country, wondering about the meaning of life and laying the groundwork for the founding of the Beatnik movement and other countercultural events since then.

Kesey, Ken
ONE FLEW OVER THE CUCKOO'S NEST

This book is the ultimate allegory of repressive institutions in America that present themselves as benevolent. Here the institution is a mental hospital, but no student can read it without recognizing that schools are a kind of loony bin too and the students "inmates." You will also find yourself unable to put down Kesey's family saga, *Sometimes a Great Notion*. It's a long one, but worth the time.

Khue, Le Minh
THE STARS, THE EARTH, THE RIVER

This collection of short stories from a master Vietnamese writer spans the era from the war period to modern times. These stories are neither rabidly anticommunist nor boringly politically correct. They simply describe real life and struggles of people in Vietnam.

Kingsolver, Barbara
POISONWOOD BIBLE

A book about missionaries in Congo, *Poisonwood Bible* has memorable characters and is a great history of colonialism in Africa. Kingsolver paints her characters with great precision and makes us understand the folly of the imperial mission to "civilize backward" peoples. She is a perennial teen favorite, with such great books as *Prodigal Summer, Bean Trees*, and *Pigs in Heaven*.

Kingston, Maxine Hong
WOMAN WARRIOR

Part *Crouching Tiger, Hidden Dragon* and part *Joy Luck Club*, *Woman Warrior* has perhaps the finest opening section of any novel I've ever read. If you love stories like Roald Dahl's *Henry Sugar*, you'll love this too. The great part about Kingston's work, which combines memoir and fiction-writing techniques, is that she begins with the mythical and then brings it home to our most mundane experiences. Is there a bit of the warrior in all of us? Kingston and I seem to think so.

Kosinski, Jerzy N.
BEING THERE

This satire of American politics is a hilarious read. A series of mis-understandings leads a "simple" man, whose only contacts with the outside world have been through television, into a dizzying ascension to political power. A fascinating parable for our times.

Kotlowitz, Alex
THERE ARE NO CHILDREN HERE

Set in a Chicago housing project, this book is a true story about two brothers; it reflects the brutal reality that many of our urban youth face every day.

Kovic, Ron
BORN ON THE FOURTH OF JULY

Kovic is a powerful ethical witness to the horrors of the Vietnam War. After joining the army right out of high school, Kovic realized that the training he got on the football field made him compliant at his insane job. Badly wounded in Vietnam, Kovic returned to the United States and went through a hellish period of rehabilitation, reassessment, and regret. He finally came to understand what had happened and became a leading peace activist.

Kozol, Jonathan
SAVAGE INEQUALITIES

This honest examination of the inequities in U.S. public schools uses a half dozen locations to expose a hypocritical system that perpetuates poverty and creates a division between the haves and the have-nots. Teenagers are moved by the stories and by Kozol's ability to balance his big-picture political analysis with the particular realities kids face daily, good and bad. Also try *Amazing Grace* and *Ordinary Resurrections*.

Krakauer, Jon
INTO THIN AIR

You won't know whether to rejoice in the adventure or shake your head in disgust at the wasted lives in this perilous venture. A true guy book, this gripping and strange story reminds me of *A Perfect Storm*, Sebastian Junger's novel about the sinking of a fishing boat, or *Blackhawk Down*, Mark Bowden's tale of war in Somalia.

Krich, John
EL BEISBOL: TRAVELS THROUGH THE PAN AMERICAN PASTIME
Travel the Latin American baseball circuit with Oaklander John Krich in this wonderfully insightful story about the passion for baseball. This book shows that the sport is widely popular in places most Americans don't even know the game exists. And, of course, a promotion to The Show of professional ball from a Dominican barrio can mean financial rescue for whole communities. If you're a baseball fan, this can stretch and deepen your sense of the game's appeal, of your sense of yourself, and of your fellow fans.

Kureishi, Hanif
GABRIEL'S GIFT
A fifteen-year-old North London boy supports his separated parents as they dream about their hippie rock-star past and realizes what it means to have a gift and to give a gift. This short novel, which provides a kid's perspective on parents and teachers, is quirky and sweet with a touch of magical realism.

Ladd, Florence
SARA'S PSALMS
In this book, a black Harvard graduate goes to Africa. She finds much more than she expected and helps us understand the realities of today's Africa. Pair this with *Zenzele*, by J. Nozipo Maraire.

Lahiri, Jhumpa
INTERPRETER OF MALADIES
This series of stories has been a best seller because it captures exquisitely the lives and struggles of modern Indians, both new immigrants and those living in India. Also check out Lahiri's *The Namesake*.

Lamb, Wally
I KNOW THIS MUCH IS TRUE
This book is a somber account of a brother dealing with his twin's mental instability. A student of mine who rarely reads has read everything that Wally Lamb has published. Lamb speaks to one's heart in a refined yet simple manner that anyone can understand. This novel is a powerfully moving account of the tragedies of real life.

Lamb, Wally
SHE'S COME UNDONE
Following Dolores Price from childhood to the age of forty, this story, which deals with many of the problems facing today's young people in a colorful way, is a lesson in endurance. Readers endure hardship and experience every emotion, but ultimately, their love for Dolores, a wickedly funny yet tragic heroine, prevails.

Lara, Adair
HOLD ME CLOSE, LET ME GO: A MOTHER, A DAUGHTER, AND AN ADOLESCENCE SURVIVED
Adair Lara writes a wonderful column in the *San Francisco Chronicle*. Here she shares lovely stories about her daughter, Morgan, and how the two survived the battles of Morgan's high school years.

Lee, Gus
CHINA BOY
This autobiographical novel begins with Kai Ting being beaten up by neighborhood bullies in the San Francisco of the 1950s. This is a moving and often funny tale of family relationships, masculine identity, boxing, and an evil stepmother.

Lee, Harper
TO KILL A MOCKINGBIRD
Author Francine Prose wrote a piece for *Harper's* disparaging Harper Lee's writing as weak prose. What was she thinking? This often-assigned book is one of the diamonds in the rough of the

high school curriculum. Scout is an enduring character with a child's-eye view of the brutal South, someone kids should get to know.

Levin, Ira
THE STEPFORD WIVES
This book is the classic exploration of the repression and control of women.

Levine, Robert
A GEOGRAPHY OF TIME
A social psychologist travels the world and describes the differences in how time is perceived, minded, and even ignored from culture to culture. This book is fascinating throughout, especially when describing how in many societies time is a way of establishing power relationships.

Lightfoot, Sara Lawrence
BALM IN GILEAD: JOURNEY OF A HEALER
This is an interesting book about multiple generations in a privileged and educated black family in New York—very much like what the Deads (in *Song of Solomon*) were trying to be had they gotten it together. It is also a great alternative to the abundance of stories about poor black folk.

Li Po and Tu Fu (trans. Arthur Cooper)
LI PO AND TU FU
This book offers gorgeous T'ang Dynasty poetry with a modern sensibility. No wonder the Beats stole from them. You will find yourself learning more from these simple poems, written around 750 AD, than from most of the obscure, pedantic modern poetry you are fed in AP English.

Maclean, Norman
A RIVER RUNS THROUGH IT
AND OTHER STORIES
For many people, this story of fathers and sons fly-fishing in western Montana is much more than a western tale—it is a meditation

on love obscured and love that is impossible to express within families. Writing toward the end of his life, Maclean looks back on his years of becoming an adult with new, and surprising, wisdom.

Maclean, Norman
YOUNG MEN AND FIRE
This novel is much more than the story of the 1949 Mann Gulch fire of Montana. In the years before fire science was invented, smoke jumpers parachuted into and hacked away at the burning brush. In this disastrous fire, fourteen young men got caught in a "blow up" and died within a few minutes. Thirty years later, near the end of his life, Maclean undertook a new investigation of the incident. His search helped solve some of the mystery and led him to a deep philosophical reflection on life, death, and everything else.

Mailer, Norman
THE NAKED AND THE DEAD
Mailer has been a literary heavy hitter for the last fifty years, and this is his finest novel. Written in 1948, this is the grittiest, most honest, and most unromanticized view of war I've ever encountered.

Maraire, J. Nozipo
ZENZELE: A LETTER FOR MY DAUGHTER
This book is a collection of moving letters from a Zimbabwean mother to a child who has gone to Harvard. The novel explores the struggles of women in Zimbabwe (then Rhodesia) and ends up offering crucial advice about life.

Maran, Meredith
DIRTY
Meredith Maran brings her personal writing style to the topic of teen drug use. She follows three teenagers who struggle with addiction in the San Francisco Bay Area for two years. Her findings, and her affection and insight for the young people, will surprise teenagers.

Márquez, Gabriel García
ONE HUNDRED YEARS OF SOLITUDE
This book is too long to read during the school year, but read it in the summer if you can't get a teacher to assign it. Gabriel García Márquez, Colombia's preeminent journalist and novelist, has done something amazing here. Sometimes teens are disconcerted by his strange narrative style, kind of distant and surfacey, until they realize that the village itself, Macondo, is the lead character and all the events in the town are part of the portrait. Radical in its style and content, *One Hundred Years* is the door to the awesome world of Latin American magical realism. Márquez's recently published autobiography, *Living to Tell the Tale,* also looks like a winner.

Martel, Yann
LIFE OF PI
This is a delightful adventure story, a Robinson Crusoe for the millennium. Teenage student Pi Patel from Pondicherry, India, is shipwrecked with a group of zoo animals, including a Bengal tiger. Martel leads one through encounters with Hindu, Christian, and Islamic philosophy.

Martinez, Manuel Luis
DRIFT: A NOVEL
This stirring novel is set in contemporary Los Angeles, bringing to life the barrios of that city while sketching a view of contemporary teen life that can apply to youths everywhere. Robert Lomos, the young protagonist, is as engaging and precocious as a Salinger hero. But he may be more accessible to those teens of today who have not been raised with East Coast privilege, boarding schools, and good suitcases

McBride, James
THE COLOR OF WATER
Fall under the spell of the intertwined stories of a mother and son in this double memoir in which jazz musician McBride shares the

stories of his unique childhood through his own telling and that of his mother. Born into a Polish Orthodox Jewish family in the 1920s, Ruth breaks out of both her family's and her society's expectations when she falls in love and marries a black man and becomes the matriarch of a large brood of lively kids.

McCall, Nathan
MAKES ME WANNA HOLLER
This autobiography of journalist Nathan McCall takes you on a fascinating journey from a black working-class neighborhood, through integrated and segregated schools, into the 1970s and the thrill of the "gangsta" lifestyle, to prison, and eventually into the professional work world. A page-turner from start to finish, this book has made readers out of nonreaders. Beware: the book has misogynistic content.

McCarthy, Cormac
ALL THE PRETTY HORSES
In this strange and affecting tale of the 1940s, two teenage boys ride south from Texas to try their luck as horse breakers in Mexico. This is like a cowboy version of *On the Road.* McCarthy has a reputation for being one of our great stylists. Note that there's a lot of violence here—never gratuitous, but sometimes horrifying.

McCormick, Patricia
CUT
Teenage self-mutilation is the subject of this engaging novel. Those who have seen the film *Thirteen* know this kind of story, but this one tells us more.

McCourt, Frank
ANGELA'S ASHES
Experience Irish poverty and struggle in this powerful, best-selling childhood memoir. McCourt startles us with his ironic and humorous eye as he comments on horrifying experiences.

McPhee, John
THE CONTROL OF NATURE
This wonderfully written book offers beautiful descriptions. McPhee is one of the best nonfiction, descriptive writers. A writer for *The New Yorker* for many years, McPhee can make any topic fascinating, even those you thought you would never read about. His other titles include *Annals of the Former World* and *Founding Fish*.

Melville, Herman
BENITO CERENO
Here is a classic novel exposing racial hypocrisy in America. A nineteenth-century merchant ship comes upon a crippled vessel with a crew decimated by illness, adrift off the coast of Chile, and filled with cowering slaves. Slowly, however, the captain realizes that the slaves have commandeered the ship and are just playacting while he inspects her. Although this is one of Melville's less popular books, it is extraordinary for its time. Many teens are also ready to handle the powerful but dense *Moby Dick*.

Miller, Henry
SEXUS
Henry Miller comes off like a jolly guy telling tall tales in the bar, but, like Samuel Johnson in the eighteenth century, he seems to capture everything about his times. Teens who read him may become better writers (and friends). *Sexus* is his best book and not all that X-rated. His most famous novel, of course, is the once-banned *Tropic of Cancer,* also a fine read.

Mistry, Rohinton
A FINE BALANCE
This book reveals deep character development in the lives of four fascinating people in India—from "untouchables" to the upper class. Mistry, who lives in Toronto, has created a great historical novel. He illuminates the period of Indira Gandhi's presidency (the mid-1970s) through the stories of the lives of common people.

Monroe, Mary
GOD DON'T LIKE UGLY
The story of an Ohio family, this new novel explores the 1960s and 1970s in the Midwest from an African American perspective.

Morrison, Toni
BELOVED
This dense novel, set during and shortly after slavery in the South and in the free city of Cincinnati, earned Morrison the Pulitzer Prize. It's also the first of her trilogy on love. *Beloved* focuses on maternal love, *Jazz* on sexual love, and *Paradise* on the love for God. Many students feel it requires two reads, and we strongly recommend that you read it with a group of friends.

Morrison, Toni
THE BLUEST EYE
Morrison's first novel reveals the devastating psychological effects of buying into unattainable (beauty) standards in the story of eleven-year-old Pecola Breedlove and her family. Like all of Morrison's novels, this book is a mixture of magical realism, deep penetration into the characters, and insights into African American life. Check out her *Sula* (see below), a novel of friendship, family, and secrets. Her most recent release is a novel simply called *Love*.

Morrison, Toni
SONG OF SOLOMON
See page 22.

Morrison, Toni
SULA
Friendships and families form the backbone of this novel, in which two girls who make up one whole become separated by adulthood. Don't be surprised if you have to reread a section or two: crazy things happen! The book has gorgeous language.

Mosley, Walter
WHITE BUTTERFLY
Mosley continues his unique and wonderful take on the mystery genre. His sometime detective Easy Rawlins is always refreshing and real, a working-class and African American recasting of the genre. Another Mosley favorite is *Always Outnumbered, Always Outgunned.*

Mosley, Walter
WORKIN' ON THE CHAIN GANG: SHAKING OFF THE DEAD HANDS OF HISTORY
In this short collection of essays about life in America in the new millennium, fiction writer Moseley really makes you think. One student gave up watching television after reading this book. It's a great read for anyone searching for meaning in our media-infested society.

Murray, Albert
TRAIN WHISTLE GUITAR
This novel, the first of a trilogy, is a prose poem incorporating the rhythms of jazz and blues into a powerful narrative style. Often those on the margins of power, in this case African Americans in Alabama, are the ones who invent a new language, a new vernacular, and new expressions—and everyone is the richer for it. Read *Stomping the Blues* for a history of blues and jazz written in that idiom.

Myles, Eileen
COOL FOR YOU
This is another harsh memoir/novel—this time about growing up working class and Catholic in Massachusetts. All the characters in these modern memoirs grow up too fast, but some describe the process beautifully.

Naylor, Gloria
MAMA DAY
Set in New York City and on a small island off Georgia populated exclusively by black folks, this love story is a classic depiction of

black female spirituality. It defies time and reality as we know it, but at the same time it is an example of how fiction can be more real than nonfiction. Also read *Linden Hills*.

Neruda, Pablo (trans. Anthony Kerrigan)
SELECTED POEMS
Well, Neruda is simply a must for everyone. This volume captures the Chilean genius's writing in a fantastic translation from the Spanish (it includes the Spanish original). Neruda captures all moods—love, depression, political outrage—with his incredible eye. Flooding readers with a series of images, Neruda's poems live in a dream state. Robert Bly writes that Neruda, "like a deep-sea crab, all claws and shell, is able to breathe in the heavy substances that lie beneath the daylight consciousness. He stays on the bottom for hours, and moves around calmly and without hysteria."

Nichols, John Treadwell
MILAGRO BEANFIELD WAR
In one of the funniest and best tales from the early 1970s, Chicano activists, hippies, and radicals team up against a huge water rip-off project. The ecological and political issues are similar to the ones we encounter today.

Nin, Anaïs
THE DIARY OF ANAÏS NIN, VOL. 1: 1931–1984
Always thoughtful, deep, and sensuous, Nin was the premier literary diarist of the 1930s. Here she carries readers to art, rebellion, and sensuality through her personal observations. Her work is extremely personal, sexy, and sensual, and it invites us to make art of our own lives.

Ninh, Bao
THE SORROW OF WAR:
A NOVEL OF NORTH VIETNAM
Bao, one of ten survivors of five hundred in the Glorious Twenty-seventh Youth Brigade of North Vietnam, has written a semi-autobiographical love story of loss and suffering. From the

Vietnamese perspective, this is what they call the American War. This book is an essential companion to any reading teens may do about the war.

O'Brian, Patrick
MASTER AND COMMANDER

You might not think that a series of books on the 1780–1820 sailing adventures of British seamen would be a grabber. But the twenty Aubrey-Maturin novels are great vacation books—you will care about the characters and enjoy this unromanticized adventure of the sailing life in the nineteenth century. It was recently made into a great Russell Crowe movie.

O'Brien, Tim
THE THINGS THEY CARRIED

See page 104.

Oe, Kenzaburo (trans. Paul St. John Mackintosh and Maki Sugiyama)
NIP THE BUDS, SHOOT THE KIDS

This book is the antidote to *Lord of the Flies*. A group of kids—juvenile delinquents and abandoned children in Japan during World War II—are left alone in an isolated area. They build a community and, in their own rough way, support each other.

Oliver, Mary
NEW AND SELECTED POEMS

Oliver writes about nature as if she's writing love poems—but without a hint of sappiness. Instead, she evokes feelings of spiritual intensity about the water, plants, and animals she describes. This is wise and beautiful writing.

Orwell, George
1984

Get the new edition of *1984*, with an introduction by Thomas Pynchon. This creepy book is about an imaginary future in which the government has launched permanent war, people are under constant surveillance, and the government speaks in something called double-speak. For some reason, everyone has started picking up this book! Check out the way Orwell anticipated today's political repression.

Pamuk, Orhan (trans. Erdag M. Goknar)
MY NAME IS RED
The noted Turkish author takes the reader on a tour of sixteenth-century Istanbul in a book that is many things at once: a suspenseful murder mystery, a romance, and a fascinating exploration of art and Islamic debates about idolatry.

Parenti, Michael
THE TERRORISM TRAP
This book can help kids make some sense of the current national crisis and uproar about the Iraq war. Parenti has encyclopedic knowledge and offers us a history of terrorism, makes connections, and provides insights. This is a most useful little handbook for these critical times.

Patchett, Ann
BEL CANTO
This powerful novel reminds us of our common humanity, even with the frightening "others," namely terrorists, taking hostages in a South American country. Flawed by its narrow perspective of the First World (wealthy countries), it is still an affecting look at human relations that should transcend political violence but seldom do.

Paul, Jim
CATAPULT
A couple of guys decide to build a medieval catapult; it turns out to be a major engineering task. Although this book is an odd, quirky, and true story, it is also an adventure in real time that may inspire many to do something interesting this summer.

Payne, C. D.
YOUTH IN REVOLT
This tale of fourteen-year-old Nick Twisp seems endlessly fascinating to teens, though most adults do not love it. Maybe the story of a runaway having his first sexual encounters does not appeal to adults. The series continues with *Revolting Youth*.

Pham, Andrew X.
CATFISH AND MANDALA
Pham embarks on an adventure and an odyssey to his past as he bicycles through Vietnam. He gives us insight into the world of Viet Kieu (Vietnamese people living away from Vietnam) and the yearning for resolution that follows the war.

Plath, Sylvia
THE BELL JAR
One of the finest examples of poetic prose available, this book shows its author's ability to craft language in the most difficult circumstances. A classic since the 1960s, it is loosely based on Plath's mental breakdown. My students love discovering how language can elegantly cut across generations to reach their souls.

Pollan, Michael
THE BOTANY OF DESIRE
Michael Pollan explores a fascinating idea: maybe plants use us as a vehicle for survival and propagation as much as we use them. Forcing us to take a look at the natural world with new eyes, Pollan devotes his chapters to different plants: apples, potatoes, tulips, and even marijuana. He also makes us think about how we see the world: as a place that needs to be ordered and tamed or as a place of wild growth and abandon.

Postman, Neil
AMUSING OURSELVES TO DEATH: PUBLIC DISCOURSE IN THE AGE OF SHOW BUSINESS
Anything by Postman will expand kids' awareness of technology and the media. Often assigned in college, Postman is readable, funny, and insightful. You will recognize thoughts you've had and complaints you've made.

Quinn, Daniel
ISHMAEL
A gorilla leads a student through long, telepathic Socratic dialogues. Quinn presents an enlightening and challenging view of the world and the so-called progress of Western civilization.

Ray, Rebbecca
PURE
Written by a sixteen-year-old high school dropout, *Pure* is narrated by a fourteen-year-old. Here Ray is dealing with rather dysfunctional hippie parents, like Saskia in *The Saskiad,* but in this case she lets herself in for physical abuse by her boyfriend in order to be popular. What's up with that? Ray works through this ugly reality to reach good insights.

Remarque, Erich Maria
ALL QUIET ON THE WESTERN FRONT
Relentless, gruesome, and horrifying, this book is the story of a group of German youths cast into the maw of World War I. This antiwar novel ranks with *Red Badge of Courage* and *Johnny Got His Gun.*

Rice, Anne
INTERVIEW WITH THE VAMPIRE
Goths and squares alike love this journey. Rice makes you think, even as she entertains you with a vampire novel. Is this an allegory of the AIDS epidemic, a mediation on death, or a heartbreaking adventure? The book is even better than the movie. Rice's other novels include *The Vampire Lestat* and *Queen of the Damned.*

Rice, Ben
POBBY AND DINGAN
This poignant story about how a young girl's imaginary friends' disappearance affects her family is beautifully narrated by her brother. Not to be missed; you will read it in one sitting.

Rice, Christopher
A DENSITY OF SOULS
When four best friends begin high school, their lifelong friendship cannot sustain the pressures of categorization. This first novel by the son of Anne Rice is a gripping mystery that involves sexuality, betrayal, and plenty of words to help kids with their SATs. Also check out his *Snow Garden.*

Robbins, Tom
EVEN COWGIRLS GET THE BLUES
This funny, quirky novel is partly a love story, partly a spiritual journey, partly an environmental treatise, and partly a philosophical pondering. A small-town girl with hitchhiker thumbs runs away from a throwaway childhood to create a meaningful life. Along the way she explores her sexuality with a Mohawk Indian, a hermit, and a lesbian cowgirl. Robbins has a knack for relating important ideas in a hilarious (if at times too hip) style.

Robbins, Tom
SKINNY LEGS AND ALL
An exploration of art, politics, and religion, this depiction of a group of inanimate objects' pilgrimage to Jerusalem might be Robbins's best. This wacky read will leave you with plenty to think about. A particularly good book to read with a group of friends.

Rochlin, Michael Jacob
AWAY GAME
This is another great baseball novel about the odyssey of a kid from the Dominican Republic who plays for the A's. Somehow all the great sports writing comes out of baseball—or at least most of it.

Rodriguez, Luis
ALWAYS RUNNING
This is one of the classic "gang memoirs," recounting *la vida loca* in East L.A. Rodriguez wrote the book as a cautionary tale, in part to try to keep his son out of gangs, and ended up creating one of the enduring classics of teen reading.

Rodriguez, Richard
HUNGER OF MEMORY
Rodriguez is often criticized for being a foe of affirmative action. But his memoir, filled with honesty and insight, defies political labeling. The author is painfully honest about his successes and sacrifices on the road toward adulthood.

Russo, Richard
EMPIRE FALLS
Capturing perfectly the pace of a small town, Russo's latest novel focuses on the events that shape our lives and our need for self-fulfillment. A winner of the 2002 Pulitzer Prize, this book provides a believable representation of high school and exposes the truth concealed behind facades of glory.

Sacco, Joe
PALESTINE
This graphic tale is a description of Sacco's experience traveling from Egypt to the Gaza Strip, the West Bank, Jerusalem, and parts of Israel. Sacco describes what he sees and holds nothing back, depicting both sides, warts and all, with powerful realism.

Sacks, Oliver
SEEING VOICES
Sacks lays out the many controversies that have wracked education for the deaf and sign language in the United States. Personal yet factual, this is a fascinating and illuminating journey. If this neurologist's great writing hooks you, look for his other amazing stories, such as *The Man Who Mistook His Wife for a Hat*, *Awakenings*, and *An Anthropologist on Mars*.

Sagan, Carl
CONTACT
Scientist Eleanor Arroway's search for extraterrestrial life leads her to examine science, faith, and her own inner life. Sagan's wide-eyed, enthusiastic face was often seen on TV as he introduced a whole generation of non-scientists to the mysteries and delights of science, especially cosmology.

Salinger, J. D.
CATCHER IN THE RYE
Once considered the preeminent teen alienation novel, this angry outburst by private school outsider Holden Caufield is now regularly taught in high schools. Although an outcast, Holden still holds his own, especially in his inarticulate grousing, which ends up being profoundly revealing.

Salinger, J. D.
NINE STORIES
In this incredible collection of short stories (yes, nine of them), the first provides another glimpse into Salinger's quirky Glass family. The book is poignant, funny, despairing, and unforgettable. Also read *Franny and Zooey*.

Santiago, Esmeralda
WHEN I WAS PUERTO RICAN
This memoir takes young Esmeralda from rural Puerto Rico to the barrios of Brooklyn, where she uses her talent to gain admission to the prestigious High School of Performing Arts. The stark contrast in cultures is stunning. Nevertheless, this book is a lovely meditation on identity in America and a positive story about family.

Sapphire
PUSH
Push is a beautiful tale told from the point of view of a retarded and abused high school girl. Here you will find, in the fog of her confusion and misinformation, a daily struggle for dignity and her redemption.

Satrapi, Marjane
PERSEPOLIS

This graphic novel takes us to a terrifying place: Iran under Aya-tollah Khomeini. Part memoir and part art project, Satrapi's work brings home the terror felt by young radicals who helped throw out the Shah of Iran and then found themselves labeled enemies by the fundamentalists.

Schlosser, Eric
FAST FOOD NATION

Thinking of picking up a Big Mac? Read this and hurl. This best seller explores the politics, economics, and nutritional impact of our drive for shortcuts and convenience.

Scoppettone, Sandra
THE LATE GREAT ME

A high school social outcast who doesn't fit in with her family finds acceptance and a first boyfriend through drinking, then suffers the consequences. Students always remark on this book's realistic and honest approach to a topic most teenagers have to deal with and how true it rings for them.

Sedaris, David
ME TALK PRETTY ONE DAY

If you're sensitive about laughing alone in public, read this book in the privacy of your own home. Sedaris's funniest collection of essays will make you howl!

Selvadurai, Shyam
CINNAMON GARDENS

World travelers have agreed that Sri Lanka, the island nation off India, is perhaps the most beautiful place on earth. This novel, set in 1927, captures the sensuous, beautiful, and painful reality of a South Asian family (Tamil Christians and Hindus) at a time when British colonial rule was under attack. A perfect summer read.

Selvadurai, Shyam
FUNNY BOY

This beautiful book is about growing up and coming out as gay in Sri Lanka. Selvadurai is an amazing artist painting pictures of life and nature that are not soon forgotten. Check out also his *Cinnamon Garden*.

Senna, Danzy
CAUCASIA

This book is one of the great novels about biracial children and a kid's eye view of the radical 1960s and early 1970s. Here is a chance for children to spy on the hypocrisies of America's racial categories. One child passes for white and learns the racist views of the white world; the other passes for black and lives in that world.

Shaara, Michael
THE KILLER ANGELS

The Killer Angels is a moment-by-moment account of the thoughts and fears of the leaders of the Confederate and Union armies during the three-day battle in Gettysburg. Shaara allows us to see the factors that tip the historical balance—sometimes courage, sometimes heroism, and at other times chance. This is a great example of historical perspective at work.

Shakespeare, William
MACBETH

For many in high school, this is the last time they will read any Shakespeare. Too bad. Because this author has been saddled with so much scholarship, we fail to recognize his wild, inventive street-theater smarts. This play is as much a psychological thriller as anything. For other accessible and powerful introductions to Shakespeare, see *The Tempest* (the one where Shakespeare imagines what kind of world we would invent if we could make a new one up) and *Hamlet* (the one with the suicide question and the challenge of when we should take action).

Silko, Leslie Marmon
CEREMONY
This is the story of Tayo, a young Pueblo Indian damaged by his experiences in a Japanese prison camp during World War II. In his search for healing, Tayo finds a profound link to his past and to the crucial rites of passage we all long for. A similar, wonderful book is M. Scott Momaday's *House Made of Dawn*. See also Silko's marvelous *Storyteller*.

Smith, Bob
HAMLET'S DRESSER: A MEMOIR
In this memoir, an unhappy, introverted teen lands a small job with a Shakespeare company and learns to process his painful life through exquisite art. This book is for budding artists, actors, and anyone who's had to find his or her meaning in a painfully alien world.

Soto, Gary
LIVING UP THE STREET
Soto's short prose-poem pieces describe a life of growing up in the barrio, playing little league baseball, and persevering.

Spiegelman, Art
MAUS
One of the early "graphic novels," this book captures one man's experience as a Jew living in Poland during World War II. The illustrations capture pain and struggle as few written works can. This book is great for kids who like to think more than they might like to read.

Steinbeck, John
EAST OF EDEN
Packed with love, lust, secrets, betrayal, miscommunication, and a history of California, this epic tale of the Trask family reads like a juicy soap opera. Don't be put off by its length—once you get into the story, you simply won't be able to put it down.

Steinbeck, John
GRAPES OF WRATH
One of the great road novels, *Grapes of Wrath* has the quintessentially American quality of being critical of and opposed to the official script of history. A group of Oklahoma white sharecroppers are driven off the land during the depression and ride in their jalopy to California, seeking the American Dream.

Steinbeck, John
OF MICE AND MEN
Friendship, shared dreams, and sacrifice are set against the background of migrant workers during the Great Depression. This book is often taught in classes and chosen by students because it is thought to be easy, that is, short. But *Of Mice and Men* is deep and enduring, presenting one of the classic innocents of fiction (Lenny) and one of the great protagonists (George).

Storm, Hyemeyohsts
SEVEN ARROWS
Seven Arrows is a book of wisdom and joy, in both form and content. Storm shares the Native American past and present in this beautiful volume, which is neither a novel nor a memoir. Rather, it seeks to break the boundaries of category, being part narrative, part artwork, part poetry, and part tales told by elders. This book is not "about" Indian culture but rather a journey to a new (for many, old) way of seeing the world.

Straight, Susan
HIGHWIRE MOON
This is a novel of desperate people, all well meaning but not always able to connect. An immigrant Mexican mother is separated from her baby when she is deported. Sixteen years later she is still trying to find her child, who is now pregnant and looking for her.

Susskind, Ron
A HOPE IN THE UNSEEN
A true story of courage, dedication, and perseverance, this moving account of Cedric, a kid who constantly battles the odds in high school and college, is both inspiring and enlightening.

Swofford, Anthony
JARHEAD
Teens can reexamine their conceptions of the first Gulf War through the memoirs of Anthony Swofford, a former marine special forces soldier. Swofford provides intense and unflinching accounts of the brutal nature of modern warfare.

Syal, Meera
LIFE ISN'T ALL HA HA HEE HEE
In this novel, Indian immigrant women in London have adventures and clashes. This book is kind of a Desai (an Indian expatriate) "Sex in the City" set in London.

Tan, Amy
THE JOY LUCK CLUB
The lives of four Chinese women in San Francisco are told over a forty-year period. You will learn the deep and profound secrets behind the determined faces of these immigrants. Also check out Tan's *Hundred Secret Senses* and *The Opposite of Fate*.

Tartt, Donna
THE SECRET HISTORY
Although this gripping suspense novel seems ridiculous at times, it thrills from start to finish. When newcomer Richard fights his way into an elite clique of classics majors at a private northeastern college, he has no idea what's in store for him. Tartt writes like a true fan of Fitzgerald but ups the ante with a plot you would never dream of.

Tayer, Jeffrey
FACING THE CONGO: A MODERN-DAY JOURNEY INTO THE HEART OF DARKNESS
Tayer is a European who decided to retrace the explorations of Henry Stanley, a nineteenth-century European explorer of Africa. Unlike Stanley, however, he brings a modern sensibility to this enduring land of the "other." Tayer's trip, like Conrad's, ends up being about self-discovery. After this book, read Conrad's *Heart of Darkness*.

Toer, Pramoedya Ananta
THIS EARTH OF MANKIND
This book is the incredible story of Minke, an Indonesian forced to reclaim his humanity from the cruelty of Dutch colonialism in the early part of the century. The story, comprising the first book of the Buru Quartet, was told to fellow prisoners while Toer was imprisoned for ten years (from 1968 to 1978).

Toole, John Kennedy
A CONFEDERACY OF DUNCES
Ignatius J. Reilly, one of the most hilarious characters you'll ever encounter, is an archetype of overblown idiocy and self-importance. Through the eyes of this unlikely hero, you'll discover the seedy underworld of the New Orleans French Quarter. When no one would publish his novel, Toole killed himself. His mother found the manuscript under his bed, brought it to a professor at Tulane, who promptly published it and made Toole famous. Was Toole the character Ignatius Reilly? Read this and decide for yourself.

Townsend, Sue
THE SECRET DIARY OF ADRIAN MOLE, AGED 13 3/4
This novel is set in England and offers a hilarious look at a pretentious and goofy young boy through his diary entries. This book

doesn't have the same tragic plot lines that many other post-*Catcher* books do. It's just a fun glimpse at a tirade against society by someone who's about to join it.

Tramble, Nichelle D.
THE DYING GROUND
The Dying Ground is a noir mystery set in 1989. The black protagonist, Maceo Redfield, is a detective by circumstance, and his friend Billy is an entry-level crack dealer who ends up dead at the corner of College and Alcatraz. This book was described as one of the first "hip hop" novels.

Traven, B.
THE JUNGLE NOVELS (THE COTTON PICKERS, THE BRIDGE IN THE JUNGLE, THE GENERAL FROM THE JUNGLE, THE REBELLION OF THE HANGED)
This series of novels by the mysterious B. Traven is gripping in its social realism. Traven (an assumed name), an Eastern European member of the Communist International, ended up living in Mexico for many years. In this series he traces the roots of the Mexican Revolution and puts real guts into proletarian fiction. His *Treasure of the Sierra Madre* was made into a famous movie starring Humphrey Bogart.

Twain, Mark
THE ADVENTURES OF HUCKLEBERRY FINN
See page 38.

Twain, Mark
THE MYSTERIOUS STRANGER AND OTHER STORIES
Written in the last years of his life, after his daughter died a tragically young death, this short novel combines Twain's searing social critiques with a compelling premise: an angel named Satan comes down to earth during the Middle Ages and appears to a

group of young Huck-like boys. Twain takes the boys (and the reader) on a wild, cynical ride through history and explores the possibilities we might all face if our lives were to change. Although technically not his best work (it ends too abruptly), kids are fascinated by the philosophical issues Twain raises.If you liked *Huck Finn*, you'd want to read his *Tom Sawyer*.

Twain, Mark
PUDD'NHEAD WILSON
This satirical novel about babies switched at birth—one is the child of a slave and the other, of a master—is a deep exploration of race in America. Once again, Twain goes to the heart of the race mythology and denigrates racists.

Tyree, Omar
A DO RIGHT MAN
In the search for a good man, sometimes you actually find one. Tyree is one of the new African American romantic novel writers. Others have enjoyed his *Flyy Girl* and *For the Love of Money*.

Valdez, Luis
LUIS VALDEZ—EARLY WORKS: ACTOS, BERNABE AND PENSAMIENTO SERPENTINO
This collection of Valdez's early work includes "Los Vendidos," a short satirical play that exposes the fallacious and stereotypical roles that Mexican Americans experience. Don't forget Valdez's classic play (made into a fine movie), *Zoot Suit*.

Verdelle, A. J.
THE GOOD NEGRESS
Twelve-year-old Denise Palms is brought from rural Virginia to Detroit to take care of her expectant mother. Toni Morrison describes this novel as "truly extraordinary."

Vonnegut, Kurt
SLAUGHTERHOUSE-FIVE
Slaughterhouse-Five is an absurd, humorous—part sci-fi and part memoir—antiwar book. In Billy Pilgrim's life, the Tralfamadori-

ans and Montana Wildhack, a porn star, coexist with the fire-bombing of Dresden in World War II. This novel was written during the disillusionment of the Vietnam period. Also check out his *Welcome to the Monkeyhouse* and *Breakfast of Champions.*

Walker, Alice
THE COLOR PURPLE

Few books can capture the pain of a naive character the way this classic by Alice Walker does. Celie's story is told through an extended series of journal entries that trace her growth from a confused, abused, and nearly illiterate young black girl to an empowered individual who has become reunited with the joys of her past. This book is a heart-wrenching must-read (*not* to be replaced by Spielberg's sappy movie version).

Walker, Margaret
JUBILEE

Here is *Gone With the Wind* told from the point of view of a black person. Life on the plantation, the end of slavery, and the humanity of all the people caught up in this social system are artfully drawn.

Wells, Rebecca
THE DIVINE SECRETS OF THE YA-YA SISTERHOOD

A New York director comes to grips with her own life and relationships when she discovers the stories of her mother's life in rural Louisiana. Tracing the zany antics of her mom and gal pals from childhood to adulthood, this book will make you laugh out loud and want to seize life!

West, Nathanael
MISS LONELYHEARTS/DAY OF THE LOCUST

These two novellas, published as a pair, are dark, funny, cynical, and every smart. *Locust* focuses on Hollywood as the epitome of the hypocrisy of the American Dream, and *Lonelyhearts* relates what happens to a man who makes himself vulnerable to the pain of people's failed dreams.

Wharton, Edith
THE HOUSE OF MIRTH
A glimpse into American upper-class society before the advent of feminism, this classic is a devastating critique of the class system written in beautiful language. Fully developed characters will leap off the pages and into your life. It takes a while to get into the book, but once you get going, you won't be able to stop.

Wideman, John Edgar
BROTHERS AND KEEPERS
Does birth order matter? Yes! Wideman, a novelist and college professor, tries to understand the difference between his life and that of his brother, who is ten years younger and who winds up in jail for murder. It's a gripping story written from shifting perspectives.

Wiesenthal, Simon
THE SUNFLOWER
On work detail as a concentration camp prisoner, Wiesenthal was asked by a dying Nazi for forgiveness. Wiesenthal said nothing. Did he do the right thing? Fifty-three political activists, theologians, and other prominent figures respond to this question, drawing on their experiences of war and conflict around the world. This book is a troubling exploration of the human capacity for forgiveness, atrocity, empathy, and conscience. What would you have done?

Williams, John A.
THE MAN WHO CRIED I AM
Williams's book is a classic of political intrigue, black revolution, a personal quest, and mystery. The main character, Max Reddrick, is fighting his own physical breakdown while also uncovering a CIA plot against black America. Williams was one of the great African American writers. Check out also *Captain Blackman*, Williams's novel of time travel to African Americans in America's wars.

Wilson, August
THE PIANO LESSON
Wilson is the greatest tragedian of our time. I may be exaggerating, but I still consider him our Shakespeare. Every few years, he has written a play set in Pittsburgh, each one in a different decade and rich with insights into African American realities, American truths, and the human soul. Other key Wilson plays include *Ma Rainey's Black Bottom* and *Fences*.

Wimsatt, William Upski
BOMB THE SUBURBS
Wimsatt is known as one of the original "hip hop journalists." In this novel, he is engaging, experimental, and youthful. You will love his riffs on everything hypocritical and everything cool in today's world. He's one of those white guys who "get it" and connect to African American culture without being cloying or patronizing.

Winchester, Simon
THE PROFESSOR AND THE MADMAN
Think dictionaries are boring? Wait until you read this tale of the seventy-year struggle to write the most incredible, comprehensive dictionary ever written, *The Oxford English Dictionary*. One of the correspondents who helped find words and references was, unbeknown to the Oxford dons to whom he was sending his work, locked up for life in a hospital for the criminally insane. See also Winchester's *Meaning of Everything: The Story of the Oxford English Dictionary*.

Wittlinger, Ellen
HARD LOVE
This book deals with interesting and alienated teens who are into publishing zines. The novel also explores unrequited love between straight and gay teenagers.

Wolff, Milton
ANOTHER HILL

Another Hill is a great autobiographical novel written by someone who has fought in the Spanish Civil War. When Wolff was eighteen years old, all the officers above him were killed, and, because he had a loud voice, he was made company commander. Wolff manages to capture the naïveté and heroism that he encountered in other young volunteers.

Wolff, Tobias
IN PHARAOH'S ARMY:
MEMORIES OF THE LOST WAR

In Wolff's memoir of his year in Vietnam, everyday absurdities show the ineffectuality of the war effort. Wolff describes Vietnam with great irony: "Here were Pharaoh's chariots engulfed; his horsemen confused; all his magnificence dismayed. A shithole."

Wolff, Tobias
THIS BOY'S LIFE

Praised by many as one of the finest memoirs of our times, *This Boy's Life* describes Wolff's many techniques for surviving as he moves away, along with his mother, from an abusive father and then has to deal with her new, abusive boyfriend. Wolff maintains a sense of humor and provides delightful insights throughout.

Wright, Richard A.
NATIVE SON

The story of Bigger Thomas, the doomed African American young man in Chicago in the 1930s, is one of the great novels of the twentieth century. Wright forces us to confront the hypocrisy of white "do-gooders" and the deeply damaged mind and character of his hero—a brutalized product of U.S. society.

Xiaolong, Qiu
DEATH OF A RED HEROINE
Inspector Chen Cao works the murder case of a famous model citizen in Shanghai. Uncovering the clues to the case, he is inexorably drawn into a pit of official corruption and has to continue his investigation while his superiors try to sabotage him.

Yoshikawa, Eiji
MUSASHI
Written in the early twentieth century, *Musashi* is the story of Miyamoto Musashi, one of the first samurai. The book combines wild swordplay with the reflective Buddhist teachings of medieval Japan—something for everyone. Although very long, this book is worth the read.

Zacks, Richard
THE PIRATE HUNTER:
THE TRUE STORY OF CAPTAIN KIDD
Before there was Enron, there were pirates who actually knew what they were doing. This is a rough-and-tumble, well-researched tale of the interlopers of early capitalism.

AUTHOR LIST

TITLE LIST

INDEX TO SUBJECT LIST

SUBJECT LIST

Titles and authors with asterisks are not included in the main list.

ABUSE AND RECOVERY

THE AFRICAN AMERICAN EXPERIENCE

THE AFRICAN AND AFRO-CARIBBEAN EXPERIENCE

ART

THE ASIAN AND ASIAN AMERICAN EXPERIENCE

BANNED BOOKS

Anaya, Rudolfo,	*Bless Me, Ultima,* 78
Atwood, Margaret,	*The Handmaid's Tale,* 123
Baldwin, James,	*Another Country,* 123
Burgess, Anthony,	*A Clockwork Orange,* 127
Burroughs, William,	*Naked Lunch,* 127
Carroll, Jim,	*The Basketball Diaries,* 128
Golding, William,	*Lord of the Flies,* 138
Huxley, Aldous,	*Brave New World,* 146
Lee, Harper,	*To Kill a Mockingbird,* 153
Morrison, Toni,	*Beloved,* 159
Morrison, Toni,	*The Bluest Eye,* 159
Morrison, Toni,	*Song of Solomon,* 22
Rodriguez, Luis,	*Always Running,* 167
Salinger, J. D.,	*Catcher in the Rye,* 168
Steinbeck, John,	*Of Mice and Men,* 172
Twain, Mark,	*The Adventures of Huckleberry Finn,* 38
Twain, Mark,	*Tom Sawyer,* 175
Vonnegut, Kurt,	*Slaughterhouse-Five,* 176
Walker, Alice,	*The Color Purple,* 177
Wright, Richard A.,	*Native Son,* 180

BIG FAT BOOKS TO TAKE ON A ROAD TRIP

Atwood, Margaret,	*The Blind Assassin,* 123
Baldwin, James,	*Another Country,* 123
Brontë, Charlotte,	*Jane Eyre,* 126
Di Prima, Diane,	*Recollections of My Life as a Woman,* 132
Eggers, Dave,	*A Heartbreaking Work of Staggering Genius,* 133
Ellison, Ralph,	*Invisible Man,* 134
Grass, Günter,	*The Tin Drum,* 141
Hughes, Langston,	*The Collected Poems of Langston Hughes,* 145

BOOKS MADE INTO GOOD MOVIES

Steinbeck, John,   *East of Eden,* 171
Steinbeck, John,   *Grapes of Wrath,* 172
Tan, Amy,   *The Joy Luck Club,* 173
Valdez, Luis,   *Zoot Suit*,* 176
Wharton, Edith,   *The House of Mirth,* 178
Wilson, August,   *The Piano Lesson,* 179

BOOKS TO TAKE TO THE BEACH
OR ON AN AIRPLANE LIGHT AND FAST

Franken, Al,   *Lies and the Lying Liars
Who Tell Them,* 136
Garland, Alex,   *The Beach,* 138
Hornby, Nick,   *High Fidelity,* 145
Robbins, Tom,   *Skinny Legs and All,* 166
Sedaris, David,   *Me Talk Pretty One Day,* 169
Wells, Rebecca,   *The Divine Secrets of
the Ya-Ya Sisterhood,* 177

BOOKS WITH LAUGHTER IN THE TITLE

Doyle, Roddy,   *Paddy Clarke Ha Ha Ha,* 133
Katzenberger, Elaine, ed.,   *First World Ha Ha Ha,* 148
Syal, Meera,   *Life Isn't All Ha Ha Hee Hee,* 173

CHICK BOOKS

Alvarez, Julia,   *How the Garcia Girls
Lost Their Accents,* 121
Brontë, Charlotte,   *Jane Eyre,* 126
Brontë, Emily,   *Wuthering Heights,* 127
Chevalier, Tracy,   *Girl with a Pearl Earring,* 129
Di Prima, Diane,   *Recollections of My Life as a Woman,* 132
Fitch, Janet,   *White Oleander,* 136
Hall, Brian,   *The Saskiad,* 142

CHILDHOOD STORIES

COMICS AND GRAPHIC NOVELS

COMING OF AGE AND GROWING UP

CULTURAL SURVIVAL

DRAMA

ENEMIES

ESSAYS THAT CAN CHANGE TEENS' LIVES

EUROPEAN FICTION

FAMILIES: BIG, SMALL, CRAZY, AND SO ON

FATHERS AND SONS

FEMINIST

FICTIONAL WAR STORIES

FRIENDS

GAY, QUEER, LESBIAN, AND TRANSGENDER

Barker, Pat, *Regeneration*, 125
Burroughs, William, *Naked Lunch*, 127
Chbosky, Stephen, *The Perks of Being a Wallflower*, 129
Fleming, Keith, *The Boy with a Thorn in His Side*, 136
Fumia, Molly, *Honor Thy Children*, 137
Irving, John, *The World According to Garp*, 146
Rice, Christopher, *Density of Souls*, 166
Rice, Christopher, *The Snow Garden**, 166
Robbins, Tom, *Even Cowgirls Get the Blues*, 166
Rodriguez, Richard, *Hunger of Memory*, 167
Selvadurai, Shyam, *Funny Boy*, 170
Tartt, Donna, *The Secret History*, 173
Wittlinger, Ellen, *Hard Love*, 179

GOTTA LAUGH TO KEEP FROM CRYING

Alexie, Sherman, *Ten Little Indians*, 120
Bambara, Toni Cade, *Gorilla, My Love*, 124
Eggers, Dave, *A Heartbreaking Work of Staggering Genius*, 133
Gogol, Nicolai, *Dead Souls*, 139
Heller, Joseph, *Catch-22*, 143
Himes, Chester, *Cotton Comes to Harlem**, 145
Himes, Chester, *Yesterday Will Make You Cry*, 145
Hornby, Nick, *High Fidelity*, 145
Irving, John, *The Hotel New Hampshire**, 146
Irving, John, *A Prayer for Owen Meany**, 146
Irving, John, *The World According to Garp*, 146
Ives, David, *All in the Timing*, 147
Kesey, Ken, *One Flew Over the Cuckoo's Nest*, 150
Kosinski, Jerzy N., *Being There*, 151
Nichols, John Treadwell, *Milagro Beanfield War*, 161
Robbins, Tom, *Skinny Legs and All*, 166
Sedaris, David, *Me Talk Pretty One Day*, 169

**GREAT BOOKS TO MAKE YOU FEEL LIKE AN EXPATRIATE
IN PARIS, SMOKING GAULOIS, AND CONTEMPLATING
EXISTENTIALIST QUESTIONS**

GREAT CHARACTERS

GUY BOOKS

HISTORICAL NOVELS

Williams, John A.,   *The Man Who Cried I Am*, 178
Yoshikawa, Eiji,   *Musashi*, 181
Zacks, Richard,   *The Pirate Hunter*, 181

HISTORY REIMAGINED

Alexie, Sherman,   *Reservation Blues*, 91
Baldwin, James,   *Notes of a Native Son**, 124
Chevalier, Tracy,   *Girl with a Pearl Earring*, 129
Galeano, Eduardo,   *Memory of Fire* (trilogy)*, 138
O'Brian, Patrick,   *Master and Commander*, 162
Twain, Mark,   *The Mysterious Stranger and Other Stories*, 175
Walker, Margaret,   *Jubilee*, 177
Williams, John A.,   *The Man Who Cried I Am*, 178
Yoshikawa, Eiji,   *Musashi*, 181

HUBRIS AND NEMESIS

Aeschylus,   *The Oresteia*, 61
Dostoyevsky, Fyodor,   *Crime and Punishment*, 133
Heaney, Seamus,   *The Cure at Troy*, 143
Melville, Herman,   *Moby Dick**, 158
Tartt, Donna,   *The Secret History*, 173

INTERESTING PAIRS: TO READ TOGETHER
OR TO HAVE TWO PEOPLE READ EACH BOOK AND COMPARE

Africa and Harvard:
Maraire, J. Nozipo, *Zenzele*, 155 and
Ladd, Florence, *Sara's Psalms*, 152

Basketball and life:
Colton, Larry, *Counting Coup*, 130 and
Joravsky, Ben, *Hoop Dreams*, 148

Teenager misunderstood (again):
Salinger, J. D., *Catcher in the Rye,* 168 and
Chbosky, Stephen, *The Perks of Being a Wallflower,* 129

INVESTIGATIVE REPORTING

Diamond, Jared,	*Guns, Germs, and Steel,* 132
Ehrenreich, Barbara,	*Nickel and Dimed,* 134
Franken, Al,	*Lies and the Lying Liars Who Tell Them,* 136
Gourevitch, Philip,	*We Wish to Inform You That Tomorrow We Will Be Killed with Our Families,* 141
Hamper, Ben,	*Rivethead,* 142
Tayer, Jeffrey,	*Facing the Congo,* 174
Katzenberger, Elaine, ed.,	*First World Ha Ha Ha,* 148
Keegan, John,	*The Face of Battle,* 149
Kotlowitz, Alex,	*There Are No Children Here,* 151
Kozol, Jonathan,	*Savage Inequalities,* 151
Krich, John,	*El Beisbol,* 152
Maclean, Norman,	*Young Men and Fire,* 155
Maran, Meredith,	*Dirty,* 155
Parenti, Michael,	*The Terrorism Trap,* 163
Susskind, Ron,	*A Hope in the Unseen,* 173

IS YOUR FUTURE FATED?

Aeschylus,	*The Oresteia,* 61
Armstrong, Karen,	*The Battle for God,* 122
Camus, Albert,	*The Stranger,* 128
Chopin, Kate,	*The Awakening,* 130
Coelho, Paulo,	*The Alchemist,* 130
Dry, Richard,	*Leaving,* 133
Fitzgerald, F. Scott,	*The Great Gatsby,* 136
Maclean, Norman,	*Young Men and Fire,* 155

JOURNEY TO ADULTHOOD

JUST CRAZY

LATINO/CHICANO AND LATIN AMERICAN EXPERIENCE

LEGACIES: THE IDENTITIES WE INHERIT FROM THE PAST

Pham, Andrew X.,   *Catfish and Mandala,* 164
Selvadurai, Shyam,   *Cinnamon Gardens,* 169
Senna, Danzy,   *Caucasia,* 170
Steinbeck, John,   *East of Eden,* 171
Tan, Amy,   *The Joy Luck Club,* 173
Wilson, August,   *The Piano Lesson,* 179
Wright, Richard A.,   *Native Son,* 180

LONERS

Alexie, Sherman,   *Ten Little Indians,* 120
Anderson, Laurie Halse,   *Speak,* 122
Burroughs, William,   *Naked Lunch,* 127
Fitzgerald, F. Scott,   *The Great Gatsby,* 136
Hulme, Keri,   *The Bone People,* 146
Katz, Jonathan,   *Geeks,* 148
Rice, Anne,   *Interview with the Vampire,* 165
Smith, Bob,   *Hamlet's Dresser,* 171

LOVE, FIRST LOVE

Alexie, Sherman,   *Reservation Blues,* 91
Alexie, Sherman,   *The Toughest Indian in the World,* 120
Alvarez, Julia,   *How the Garcia Girls Lost Their Accents,* 121
Bloch, Ariel and Chana,   *The Song of Songs,* 126
Brontë, Charlotte,   *Jane Eyre,* 126
Brontë, Emily,   *Wuthering Heights,* 127
Chbosky, Stephen,   *The Perks of Being a Wallflower,* 129
Escandón, María Amparo,   *Esperanza's Box of Saints,* 135
Faulks, Sebastian,   *Birdsong,* 135
Fitzgerald, F. Scott,   *The Great Gatsby,* 136
Hemingway, Ernest,   *The Sun Also Rises*,* 143
Hornby, Nick,   *High Fidelity,* 145
Hulme, Keri,   *The Bone People,* 146

MAGICAL REALISM

MEMOIRS

THE MIDDLE EAST AND SOUTH ASIA

MUSIC AND MUSICIANS

MYSTERY

Okay, we left out the classics here, like Chandler and Hammett. But here are some unique and interesting ones.

NATIVE AMERICAN EXPERIENCE

Alexie, Sherman,	*The Lone Ranger and Tonto Fistfight in Heaven*, 120
Alexie, Sherman,	*Reservation Blues*, 91
Alexie, Sherman,	*Ten Little Indians*, 120
Alexie, Sherman,	*The Toughest Indian in the World*, 120
Castellanos, Rosario,	*The Nine Guardians*, 128
Colton, Larry,	*Counting Coup*, 130
Dorris, Michael,	*A Yellow Raft in Blue Water*, 132
Erdrich, Louise,	*The Beet Queen**, 134
Erdrich, Louise,	*The Birchbark House**, 134
Erdrich, Louise,	*Love Medicine**, 134
Erdrich, Louise,	*Tracks*, 134
Hillerman, Tony,	*The Wailing Wind*, 144
Momaday, M. Scott,	*House Made of Dawn**, 171
Morrison, Toni,	*Song of Solomon*, 22
Silko, Leslie Marmon,	*Ceremony*, 171
Storm, Hyemeyohsts,	*Seven Arrows*, 172

NATURE WRITING

Berry, Wendell,	*Life Is a Miracle*, 125
Berry, Wendell,	*Sex, Economy, Freedom, and Community**, 125
Berry, Wendell,	*The Unsettling of America**, 125
Berry, Wendell,	*What Are People For?**, 125
McPhee, John,	*Annals of the Former World**, 158
McPhee, John,	*The Control of Nature*, 158
McPhee, John,	*Founding Fish**, 158
Pollan, Michael,	*The Botany of Desire*, 164

PARALLEL UNIVERSES OF HUMAN EXPERIENCE

PARENTS, IMPERFECT

PHILOSOPHY, DEEP AND SHALLOW

POETRY AND BOOKS ABOUT POETRY

THE POLITICAL STRUGGLE FOR FREEDOM

THE *RASHOMON* EFFECT: FICTION AND NONFICTION TOLD FROM SHIFTING PERSPECTIVES

RELIGION

Alexie, Sherman,	*Reservation Blues,* 91
Armstrong, Karen,	*The Battle for God,* 122
Armstrong, Karen,	*The History of God*,* 122
Armstrong, Karen,	*Islam*,* 122
Berry, Wendell,	*Life Is a Miracle,* 125
Diamant, Anita,	*The Red Tent,* 131
Gaiman, Neil,	*American Gods,* 137
Goldberg, Myla,	*Bee Season,* 140
Haley, Alex,	*The Autobiography of Malcolm X,* 142
Hesse, Hermann,	*Siddhartha,* 144
Hulme, Keri,	*The Bone People,* 146
Martel, Yann,	*Life of Pi,* 156
Morrison, Toni,	*Song of Solomon,* 22
Pamuk, Orhan,	*My Name Is Red,* 163
Robbins, Tom,	*Skinny Legs and All,* 166
Silko, Leslie Marmon,	*Ceremony,* 171

SCIENCE, ECOLOGY, AND COSMOLOGY

Berry, Wendell,	*Life Is a Miracle,* 125
Berry, Wendell,	*Sex, Economy, Freedom, and Community*,* 125
Berry, Wendell,	*The Unsettling of America*,* 125
Berry, Wendell,	*What Are People For?*,* 125
Gould, Stephen Jay,	*The Hedgehog, the Fox, and the Magister's Pox,* 140
Levine, Robert,	*A Geography of Time,* 154
McPhee, John,	*Annals of the Former World*,* 158
McPhee, John,	*Founding Fish*,* 158
Paul, Jim,	*Catapult,* 163
Pollan, Michael,	*The Botany of Desire,* 164
Postman, Neil,	*Amusing Ourselves to Death,* 165

Sacks, Oliver,   *Awakenings*, 167*
Sacks, Oliver,   *The Man Who Mistook*
                 His Wife for a Hat*, 167
Sacks, Oliver,   *Seeing Voices, 167*
Schlosser, Eric,   *Fast Food Nation, 169*

SCIENCE FICTION AND FANTASY

This is not an insider's guide to science fiction and fantasy, subjects on which teenagers are often the experts. Consider these more as points where fantasy and science fiction overlap with other categories. There's a vast literary world just beyond this list.

Alexie, Sherman,   *The Toughest Indian in the World, 120*
Atwood, Margaret,   *The Handmaid's Tale, 123*
Bradbury, Ray,   *Fahrenheit 451, 126*
Burgess, Anthony,   *A Clockwork Orange, 127*
Butler, Octavia,   *Kindred*, 127*
Butler, Octavia,   *Parable of the Talents, 127*
Dick, Philip,   *Do Androids Dream*
               of Electric Sheep?*, 132
Dick, Philip,   *Man in the High Castle, 132*
Dick, Philip,   *A Scanner Darkly*, 132*
Dick, Philip,   *The Simulacra*, 132*
Herbert, Frank,   *Dune, 144*
Huxley, Aldous,   *Brave New World, 146*
Kay, Guy Gavriel,   *Tigana, 149*
Levin, Ira,   *The Stepford Wives, 154*
Orwell, George,   *1984, 162*
Quinn, Daniel,   *Ishmael, 165*
Sagan, Carl,   *Contact, 168*
Vonnegut, Kurt,   *Breakfast of Champions*, 176*
Vonnegut, Kurt,   *Slaughterhouse-Five, 176*
Vonnegut, Kurt,   *Welcome to the Monkeyhouse*, 176*

SEX

See also Love; yes, there's a difference.

Ackerman, Diane, *A Natural History of the Senses,* 119
Alexie, Sherman, *The Toughest Indian in the World,* 120
Berry, Wendell, *Sex, Economy, Freedom,*
and Community*, 125
Carroll, Jim, *Basketball Diaries,* 128
Miller, Henry, *Sexus,* 158
Miller, Henry, *Tropic of Cancer*,* 158
Nin, Anaïs, *The Diary of Anaïs Nin,* 161
Payne, C. D., *Youth in Revolt,* 164
Rice, Christopher, *A Density of Souls,* 166
Robbins, Tom, *Even Cowgirls Get the Blues,* 166

SHORT BOOKS, QUICK READS

Apollo, *Concrete Candy,* 122
Block, Francesca Lia, *Weetzie Bat,* 126
Bradbury, Ray, *Fahrenheit 451,* 126
Carroll, Jim, *The Basketball Diaries,* 128
Chbosky, Stephen, *The Perks of Being a Wallflower,* 129
Gaines, Ernest J., *A Gathering of Old Men,* 138
Kaysen, Susanna, *Girl, Interrupted,* 149
Kosinski, Jerzy N., *Being There,* 151
Rice, Ben, *Pobby and Dingan,* 166
West, Nathanael, *Miss Lonelyhearts/Day of the Locust,* 177

SHORT STORIES

Alexie, Sherman, *The Lone Ranger and Tonto*
Fistfight in Heaven, 120
Alexie, Sherman, *Ten Little Indians,* 120
Alexie, Sherman, *The Toughest Indian in the World,* 120

SIBLINGS, SIBLING RIVALRIES

THE SOUTH

SPIRITUAL JOURNEYS

SPORTS

TALKING BACK: MAKING MORAL CHOICES IN AN IMMORAL WORLD

TEENAGE ALIENATION AND REBELLION

TRUE WAR STORIES

URBAN GRITTY

CONTRIBUTORS

Rick Ayers teaches English at Berkeley High School in California. He is the coordinator of that school's Communication Arts and Sciences program. With a master's in education from Mills College, Ayers has taught curriculum at California State University, Hayward; Mills College; and the University of San Francisco. He is co-editor of *Zero Tolerance: Resisting the Drive for Punishment, A Handbook for Parents, Students, Educators and Citizens* and author of *Studs Terkel's* Working: *A Teaching Guide*.

Dean Woodring Blase studied comparative literature at the University of Michigan's Residential College and holds degrees from Miami University and the Bread Loaf School of English. She teaches English in Cincinnati, Ohio, where she works at the nation's first public Montessori high school. She is a National Board Certified teacher and is the founder of Sprockets, a student film festival.

Amy Crawford received her B.A. in Italian literature and African American studies from the University of Wisconsin and spent a year studying in Bologna, Italy. She earned a master's degree in education from Mills College. She has taught in the Bay Area since 1995, and she currently teaches English in the Communication Arts and Sciences program at Berkeley High School.

Emily Donaldson grew up intently observing her teachers and is now herself a teacher. After receiving her B.A. in English and African American studies from Columbia, Emily returned to her own public high school to teach English for three years. She now teaches in the largest town in the United States, Framingham, Massachusetts. Emily hopes to help kids enjoy thinking closely about what they read, see, and hear, as they help her, for many years to come.

Lauren Hennessey Jackson graduated from Haverford College and the University of Pennsylvania. She has taught English and interdisciplinary humanities courses on Bainbridge Island, Washington, and at Hong Kong International School. Teaching American Studies with Alan James and Susan Crossley has changed her understanding of how students learn and of her role as a teacher. She aims to expose kids to the forces that affect literature and to focus on what students understand rather than what they know.

For the past fifteen years **Alan James** has been teaching Russian language, social studies, and, more recently, interdisciplinary courses in a variety of independent schools. He currently teaches at Hong Kong International School. A graduate of Dartmouth College, the University of Washington, and Teachers College, Columbia University, his academic focus has been on Russian language, comparative European history, and U.S. foreign policy. He learned everything he knows about teaching writing and literature within an interdisciplinary mode from his teaching partners at HKIS, including the coauthor of his article, Lauren Jackson.

Bonnie Katzive has taught English/language arts since 1993. She has a B.A. in art and archeology from Washington University in St. Louis as well as an M.A. in history of art and a Bay Area Writing Project Teaching Credential from UC Berkeley. Bonnie currently teaches ninth- and tenth-grade core literature and composition classes as well as mythology at Monarch High School in Louisville, Colorado. She is at work on a set of poems intertwining mythology with the (imagined) inner life of inanimate objects.

Sarah Talbot attended The Evergreen State College and Seattle University. She lives, writes, and teaches in Olympia, Washington, home of the fighting geoducks and other atrocities. Sarah has been teaching English for eight years, mothering for thirteen, and writing for thirty. She has written for several periodicals, including *HipMama* and *Rag* magazines, and is currently working on a fictional exploration of maternal insanity.

ACKNOWLEDGMENTS

Rick thanks the following family, friends, and students for their encouragement, challenges, and bright ideas for this project:

Bill Ayers, Ilene Abrams, Aisha Ayers, William Lovatt, Mona Khalidi, Melissa Mytinger, Jim Burke, Chinaka Hodge, Peter and Joanna Letz, and Julio Rodriguez.

Amy extends her deepest thanks and appreciation to the following folks for their help and support in this project:

Robin Kurzer, Whitney Blakemore, Dean Blase, Lynn Crawford, Bill Crawford, Anne Crawford, Richard Crawford, Penelope Crawford, Linda Crawford, Morgan Karan-Harwin, Rachel Schaffran, Tatiana, Anneka, Kate, Sonya, Sarah, Sherry, Sonia, Lauren, Alena, Emily, Meggy, Kris, Kate O'Hara, Daniel Palau, Dana Rosenberg, Daniel Palau, Sue Whitaker, Dick Whitaker, Liza Engelberg, and, most of all, Richard Whitaker.

And we both thank our wonderful editor at Beacon, Andy Hrycyna.